A Note From the Author

Dear Theory student,

Congratulations! You have just done the very best thing for your theory education — you've bought this book.

This completely-up-to-date edition of How to Blitz! Theory Grade 1 contains more information, more revision and more worksheets than any other theory text book.

One of the best features is the clearest and easiest section on music notation ever written. It assumes you've never actually seen music before. If you already know how to read music, you will find this section SUPER EASY!!! Whizz through it and impress all your friends.

You'll see there are lots of keyboard diagrams in this book. This is because the piano keyboard is a visual pattern and is the most helpful in demonstrating certain things you need to learn, such as semitones and accidentals. If you are learning to play an instrument other than piano, you'll find that these keyboard diagrams help you understand some of the concepts more easily.

So, have fun and enjoy working through this book. Every time you see this icon it means there are more practice examples you can download from the BlitzBooks website. Go to blitzbooks.com to download FREE manuscript, flashcards, worksheets and more!

Happy Theory-ing,

Samantha

ISBN 1-877011-31-2
First edition published 2001 by BlitzBooks Pty Ltd
Copyright © Samantha Coates
Reprinted by Markono Print Media November 2024

A mountain of thanks to: my fabulous friends, students and colleagues for their wonderful advice and unfailingly accurate proof-reading; to my gorgeous children for putting up with me in those early years; and of course to my brilliant husband Andrew, without whom there would simply be no books.

Table of Contents

A Little Bit About Rhythm 3

Intro to Pitch 4

Clefs, Notes, and Stems 7

Leger Lines 12

Revision of Stuff So Far 13

Sharps, Flats and Naturals 14

Naming and Drawing Notes 18

Tones, Semitones and the Major Scale 22

Scale Degree Numbers 24

Tiny Test 28

Scales with Accidentals/Scale Worksheets 29

Timed Test 35

Naming the Key/More on Scale Degrees 36

Intervals 40

Revision of Heaps of Things 43

Tonic Triads 44

Very Important Revision Test 46

Time and Rhythm 48

The Anacrusis 51

Grouping 53

Completing the Bar 55

Another Test on Stuff 58

Transposition 60

Word Search 65

Terms and Signs 66

Timed Test II 68

More About Signs 69

Final Revision Test 71

Mad Multiple Choice 72

Test Paper... sort of 75

A Little Bit About Rhythm

Here is a tiny introduction to the different ways music notes are written. The shape of a note determines its length, or number of 'beats'. Heaps more about this later on... plus you can visit **blitzbooks.com** for excellent rhythm games such as Beat Bingo!

Note	Name	Number of Beats
o	Semibreve	4
𝅗𝅥.	Dotted Minim	3
𝅗𝅥	Minim	2
♩	Crotchet	1
♪	Quaver	$\frac{1}{2}$
♪ + ♪ = ♫	Two quavers joined	$\frac{1}{2} + \frac{1}{2} = 1$
♪ + ♪ + ♪ + ♪ = ♬	Four quavers joined	$\frac{1}{2} + \frac{1}{2} + \frac{1}{2} + \frac{1}{2} = 2$

In music there are also symbols to show lengths of silence. These are called RESTS.

Rest	Name	Number of Beats
𝄻	Whole bar rest/Semibreve rest	Depends on time signature*
𝄼	Minim rest	2
𝄽	Crotchet rest	1
𝄾	Quaver rest	$\frac{1}{2}$

*See page 48 for info on time signatures

Here is a rhythm quiz. Add up the beats!

1. 𝅗𝅥 + 𝅗𝅥. = ___
2. ♩ + 𝄾 = ___
3. ♬ + 𝅗𝅥 = ___
4. ♫ + 𝄽 = ___
5. ♩ + ♩ + ♫ = ___
6. o + 𝅗𝅥 = ___
7. ♫ + 𝅗𝅥. = ___
8. 𝄾 + 𝄼 + ♪ = ___

Introduction to Pitch Notation

As well as rhythm, music has pitch - sounds that are high, middle or low. Pitch is shown on sets of 5 lines, called a 'staff' or 'stave'. We'll refer to it both ways throughout this book. Here are some semibreves on a stave:

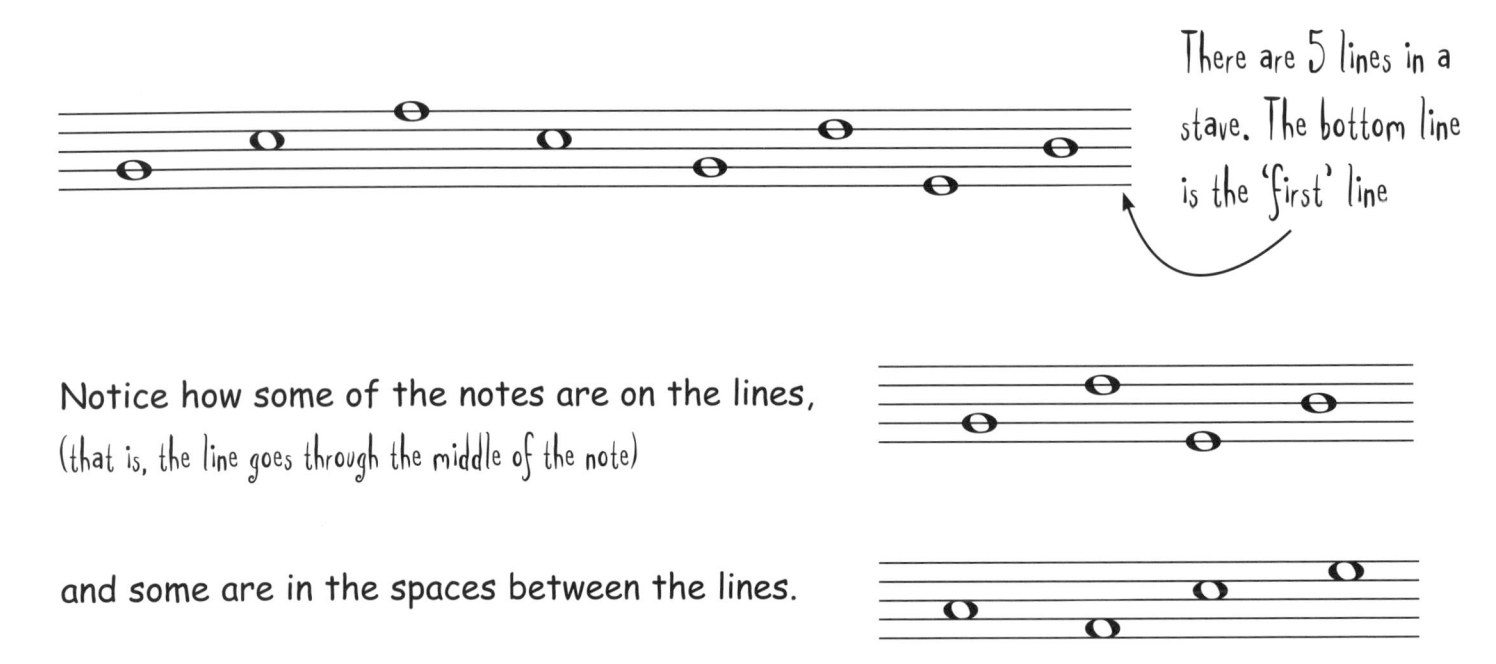

There are 5 lines in a stave. The bottom line is the 'first' line

Notice how some of the notes are on the lines, (that is, the line goes through the middle of the note)

and some are in the spaces between the lines.

Piano music is actually written on two staves bracketed together, called a 'grand stave':

Treble clef, used for notating high-pitched notes

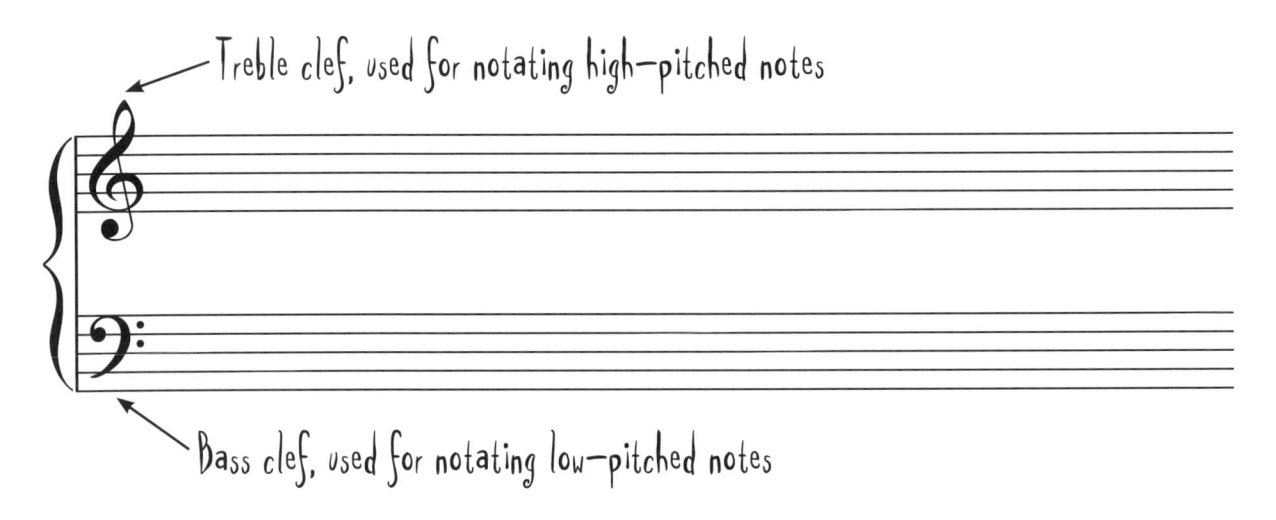

Bass clef, used for notating low-pitched notes

Draw some semibreves on the grand stave above. Put some in the treble, some in the bass, some on the lines and some in the spaces! (oh dear that actually nearly rhymes)

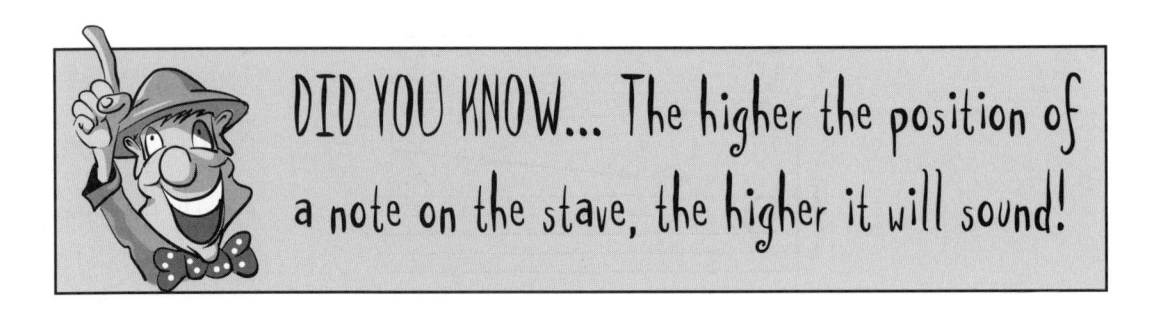

DID YOU KNOW... The higher the position of a note on the stave, the higher it will sound!

The (Unofficial) Story of Middle C

Once upon a time, music used to be written on 11 lines, like this:

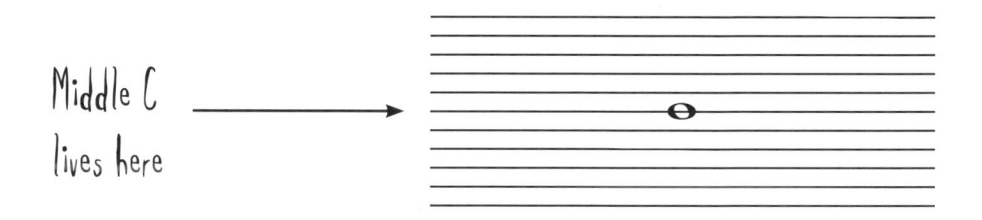

Middle C lives here ⟶

The note named 'C' lived on the line right in the middle. It was called 'Middle C'.

Many people found it very confusing looking at 11 lines all the time, and found it even more confusing trying to find Middle C. Then one day, somebody came up with the idea of taking out the middle line, leaving 2 sets of 5 lines.

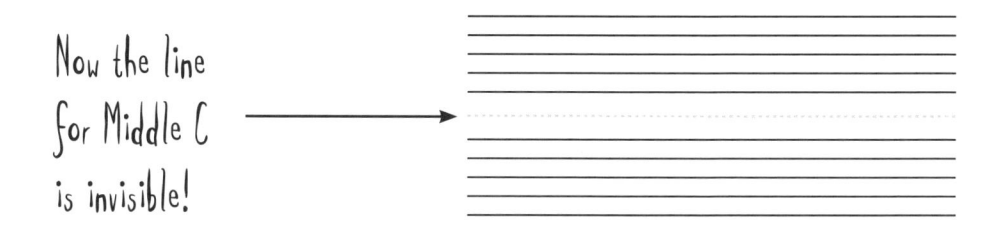

Now the line for Middle C is invisible! ⟶

This was much easier to look at! Then look what happened:

The two sets of lines were moved even further apart; the top set was given a treble clef and the bottom set a bass clef, leaving space for Middle C in between. And so the grand stave was born!

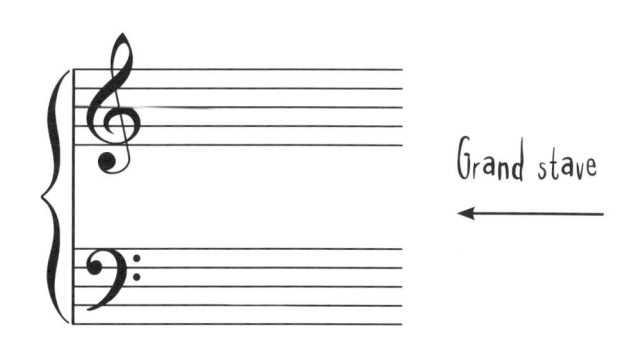

Grand stave ⟵

It was decided that Middle C would need its own short line, called a 'leger line'. Middle C is always written close to either bass or treble, never floating in between.

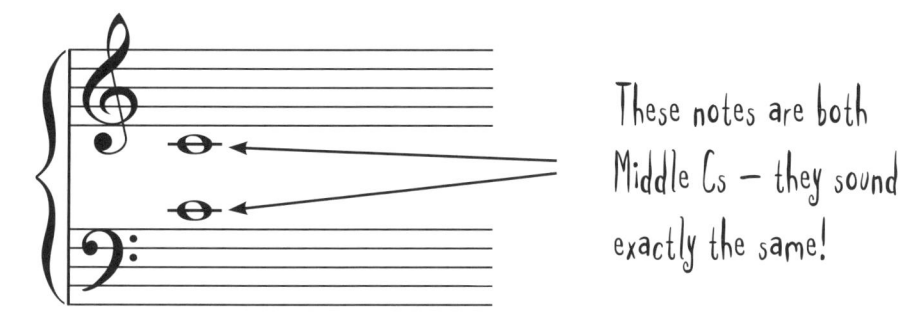

These notes are both Middle Cs — they sound exactly the same!

Some instruments, like the flute, are high-pitched, which means they mostly play notes above Middle C. These instruments only need a treble clef to show their notes:

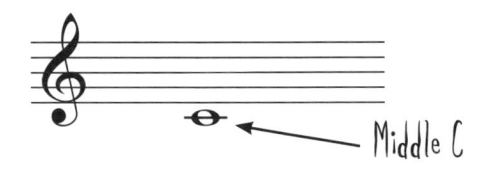

Other instruments, like the trombone, are low-pitched, which means they mostly play notes below Middle C. These instruments only a need bass clef to show their notes:

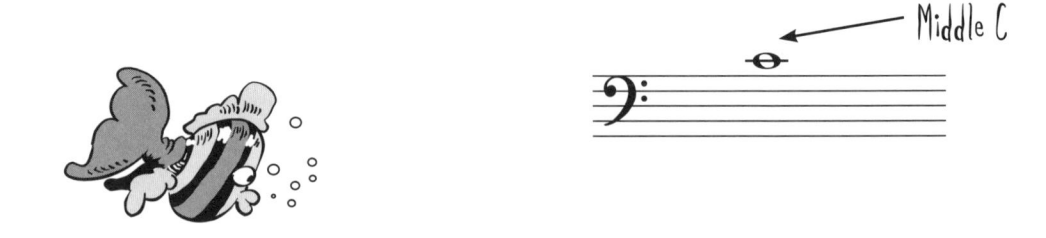

A piano has the largest range of sounds of any musical instrument, so it needs a 'grand stave' to show all the notes. You will notice that the names of the notes are the same as the first seven letters of the alphabet, repeated over and over again:

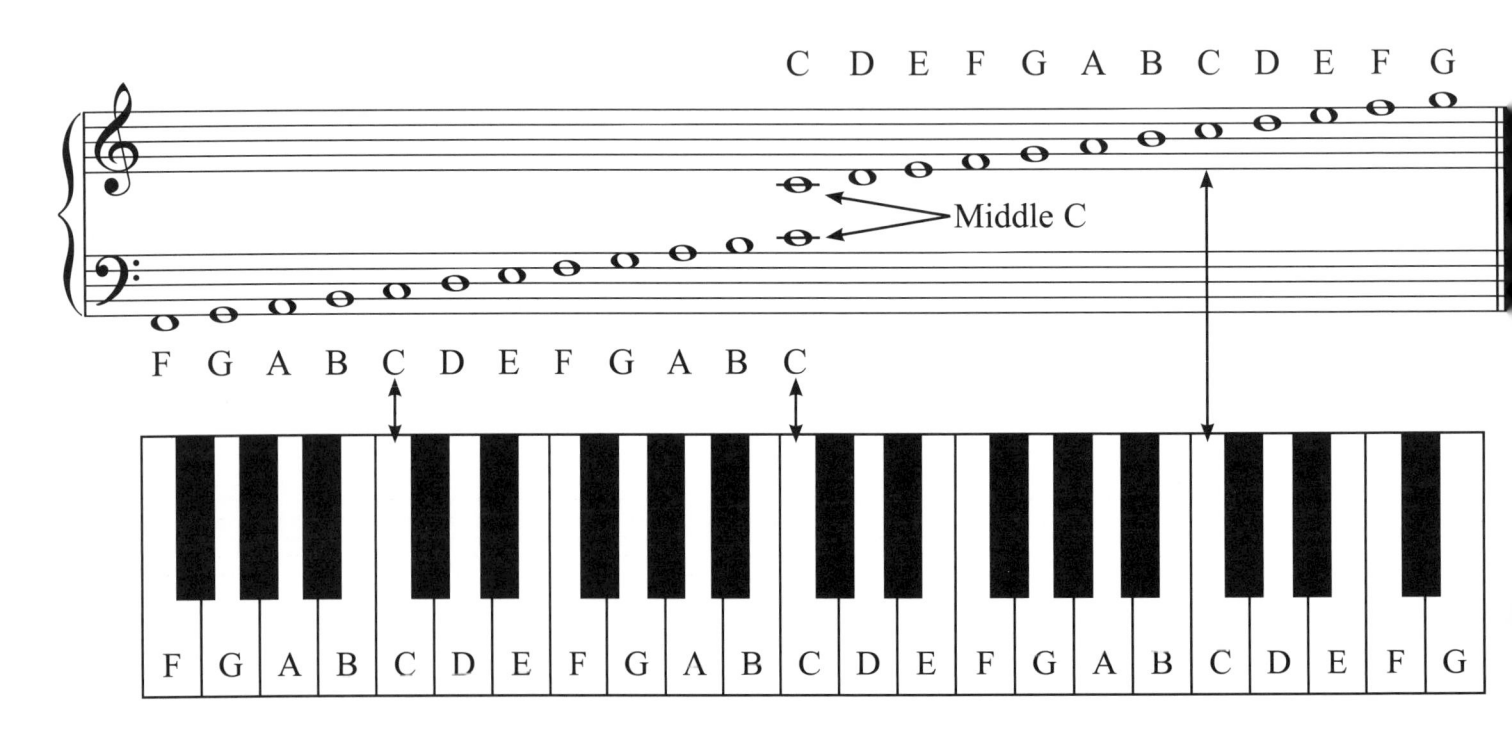

FACT: The piano keyboard has even more keys than this, but we've run out of room on the grand stave! Extremely high or extremely low notes are written using 'leger lines'. (see p.12)

Drawing Treble and Bass Clefs

Treble clef starts on the line where G lives , then winds around like this . Then it goes up and makes a loop above the staff and as it comes down it intersects on the 4th line . (Very important!)

Trace these treble clefs and then draw some of your own.

The bass clef starts on the line where F lives , then curls around like a backwards 'c' , stopping just before the bottom line. Then two dots are added either side of the fourth line . (Also very important!)

Trace and draw some bass clefs here.

HERE'S A THOUGHT... The treble clef used to be called the G clef and the bass clef used to be called the F clef. Can you figure out why?

Treble Clef Notes

You can work out the names of all the notes in the treble from G. Fill in the rest!

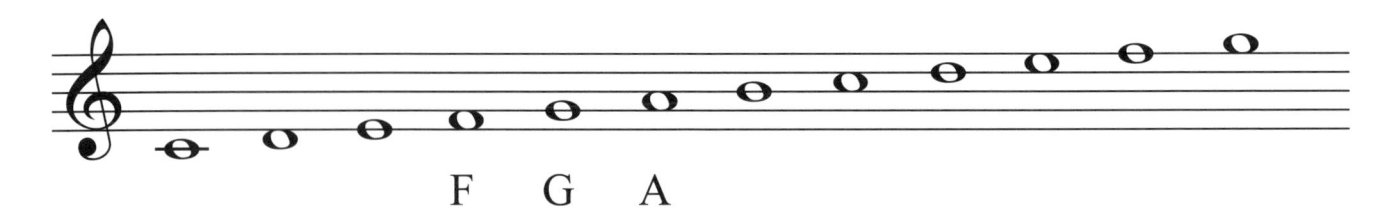

F   G   A

Quick Quiz:

How many are named F? ___ Which F is on a line, the lower F or the higher F? _____

Name 4 different notes you can see that live in spaces. ___ ___ ___ ___

There are 2 notes named E, the lower E is on a _____, the higher E is in a _____.

There are 2 notes named D, the lower D is in a _____, the higher D is on a _____.

(P.S. If the note is sitting above or hanging below the stave, it's still 'in a space')

Can you name these notes? (Without peeking at the top of the page???)

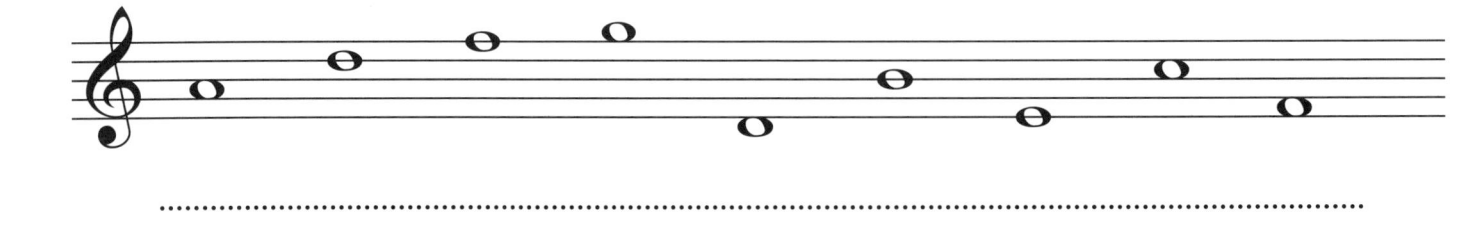

And now, can you write these notes? Draw a new treble clef in every bar!

F on a line   G in a space   A in a space   D on a line

G on a line   C on a line   E in a space   D in a space

Bass Clef Notes

Similarly, you can work out the names of all the bass notes from F on the fourth line...

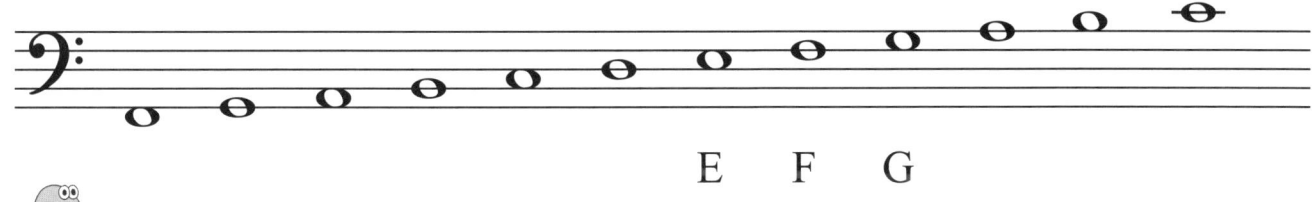

E   F   G

Name these notes. (Remember that F lives on the fourth line – you can work out all the other notes from there!)

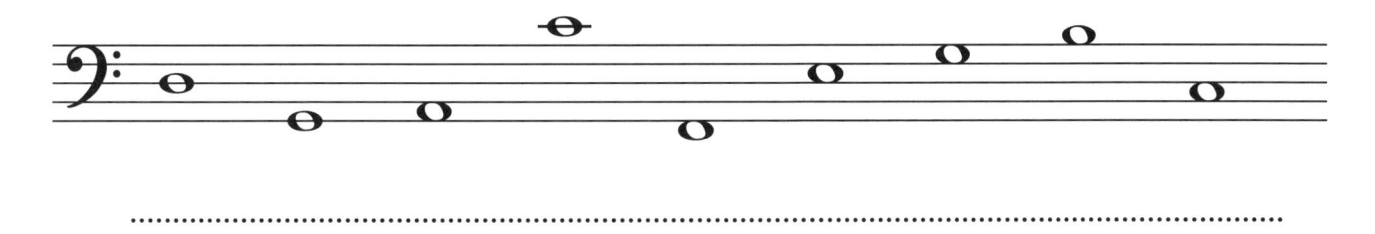

....

And now, draw a bass clef in each new bar and write the following notes:

A in a space   D on a line   A on a line   C in a space

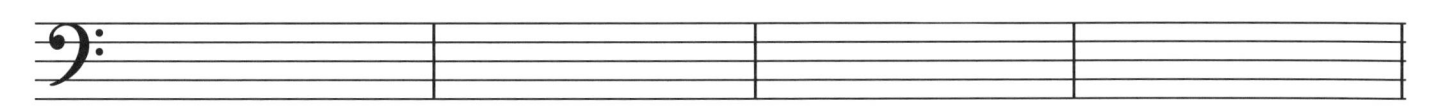

B in a space   F on a line   G on a line   E in a space

QUICK REVISION:

Draw Middle C for treble clef here:

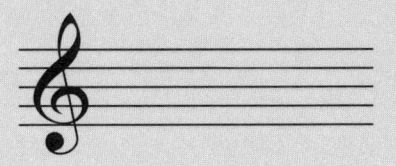

Draw Middle C for bass clef here:

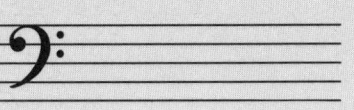

9

Drawing Notes with Stems

So far we've only been using semibreves (o) to draw notes on staves. Now we're going to use other note values, which have stems (𝅗𝅥. 𝅗𝅥 ♩) and sometimes tails too (♪).

A stem can go up (♩) on the right side of the note, or down (♩) on the left side. The direction of the stem depends on where the note sits.

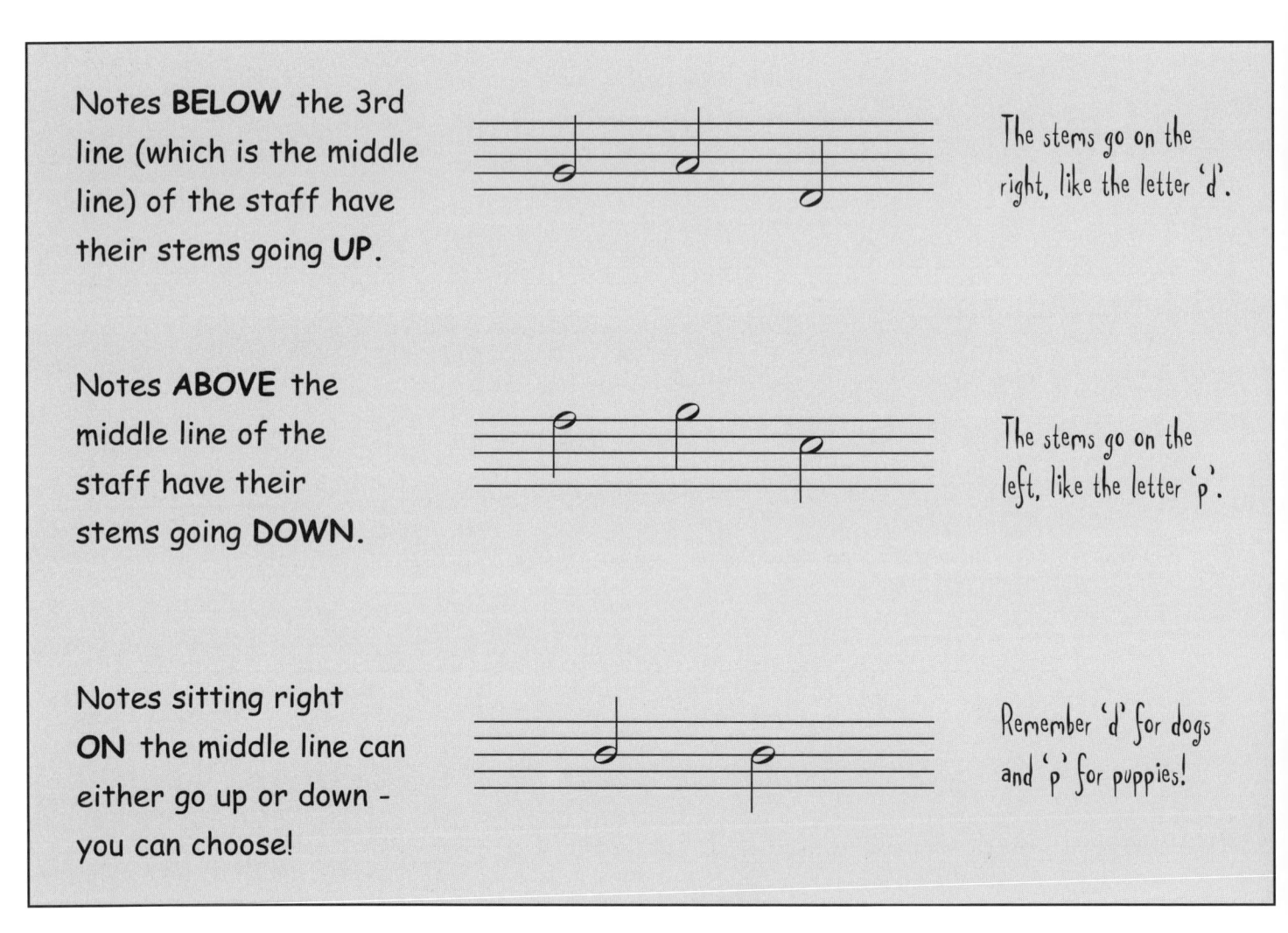

Notes BELOW the 3rd line (which is the middle line) of the staff have their stems going **UP**.

The stems go on the right, like the letter 'd'.

Notes ABOVE the middle line of the staff have their stems going **DOWN**.

The stems go on the left, like the letter 'p'.

Notes sitting right ON the middle line can either go up or down - you can choose!

Remember 'd' for dogs and 'p' for puppies!

Handy Hint: Stems should always reach to the next note of the same letter name, e.g.

is too short but

The next 'E' lives here

is just right!

1. Make these note heads into minims by adding stems in the correct direction. Remember 'd' for dogs and 'p' for puppies!

2. Now add a dot to each note to make all the minims above into dotted minims. (If the note is on a line, draw the dot in the space just above, otherwise we won't see it!)

3. Make these note heads into crotchets. You'll need to colour them in AND add stems!

4. Make the following into quavers by adding a stem and a tail (♪ or ♪). The tail always goes forwards (to the right) even if the stem is going down.

5. Two quavers can be joined together by a 'beam', e.g. or Both stems MUST go in the same direction. For pairs of notes where one stem would go up and the other down, e.g. , the note furthest from the middle line 'wins', like this: !

Make these note heads into pairs of quavers. Draw the stems first, then add 'beams'.

11

Leger Lines

Leger lines are miniature staff lines used to show very high or very low notes. In Grade 1 you're only tested on notes with one or two leger lines above or below the stave, but there's actually no limit to how many you can use in general music!

Wow! What note is THAT???

Here are some treble notes on leger lines. All of these are referred to as notes 'above' or 'below' the staff. (The notes in grey are not leger line notes, but they are also referred to as 'D below the staff' etc.)

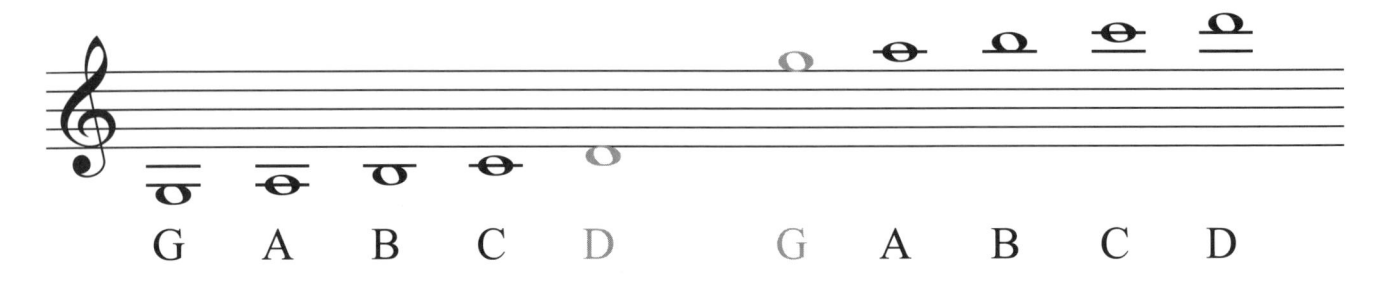

G A B C D   G A B C D

And now here are the bass notes that live 'above' or 'below' the staff:

B C D E F   B C D E F

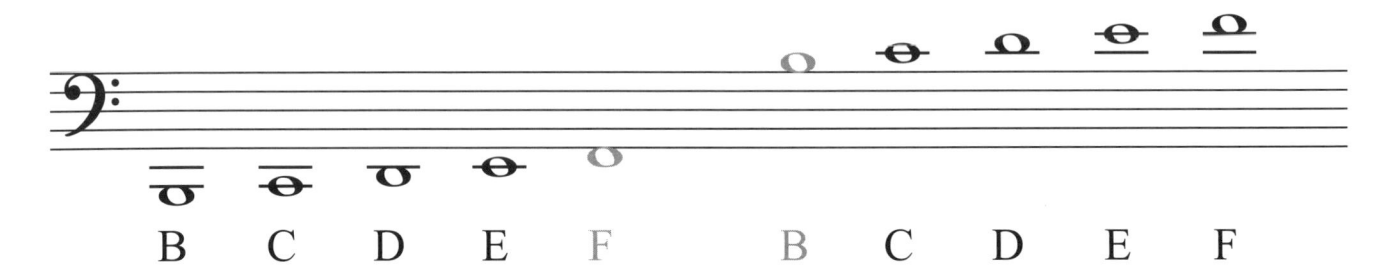

Notes that hang from leger lines look like this o NOT this ⊻ – no 'shoe' needed!

Notes that sit on leger lines look like this o NOT this ⊼ – no 'hat' needed!

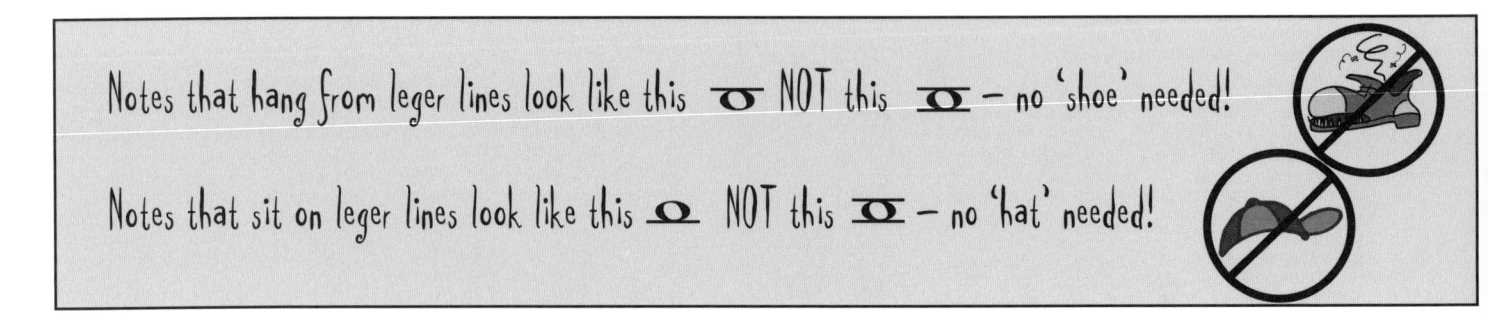

When drawing leger lines, keep them spaced the same distance apart as the staff lines. Draw the line or lines first, then draw the note! Trace these then draw your own...

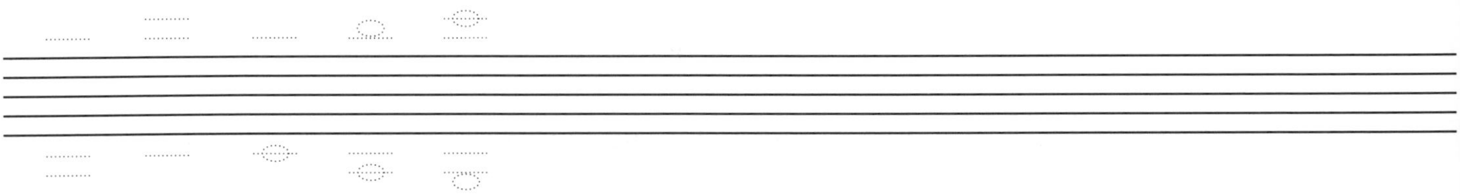

Revision of Stuff So Far

1. Write the following notes **above** the stave (watch out for clef changes):

   C   D   A   G

2. Write the following notes **below** the stave (again, watch out for clef changes):

   D   E   C   B

3. ♩ + ♫ + 𝄻 + ♩. + 𝄽 + 𝅝 = ____ beats?

4. Draw these notes **and clefs**:

   A in 3 places in the **treble**   D in 3 places in the **bass**

5. Make the notes in questions 1 and 2 into minims.

6. Make the notes in question 4 into separate quavers.

7. Make the notes in question 6 into hemidemisemiquavers. (Just checking you are paying attention)

Sharps, Flats and Naturals (a.k.a. 'Accidentals')

Sharp (♯), flat (♭) and natural (♮) signs are known as 'accidentals'. They are used to change the pitch of a note. Each of these signs will change the pitch by one 'semitone'. **A semitone is the distance between a note and its nearest neighbour.**

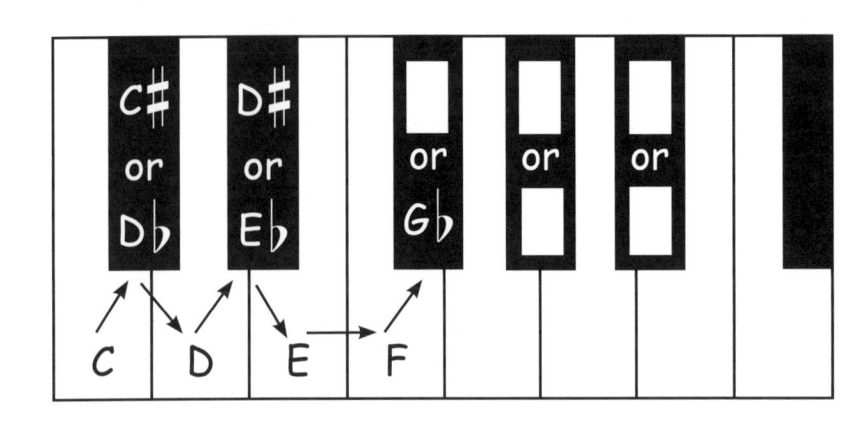

On a piano keyboard, the semitones are very easy to see. The arrows show the steps by semitones. C to C♯ is a semitone. E to F is also a semitone. See if you can fill in the rest of the names and arrows!

An accidental before a note will change the way it sounds:

G sharp sounds one semitone higher than G.

G flat sounds one semitone lower than G.

G natural is the same as G - a natural sign cancels out a sharp or flat sign.

DID YOU KNOW... Accidentals are always written BEFORE the note? So even though we say 'G-sharp', we write 'Sharp-G'!

Play some notes with accidentals on your instrument. Notice how D♯ sounds the same as E♭, G♯ sounds the same as A♭, etc. Don't forget to try E♯ - it sounds the same as F! How about B♯? And what about C♭? Notes have more than one name... just like you do!

Quick Quiz:

♯ = _____ sign = note sounds one semitone _____

♭ = _____ sign = note sounds one semitone _____

♮ = _____ sign = cancels out a _____ or a _____ sign

Sharps, flats and naturals can be tricky to draw. They must sit on exactly the same line or in exactly the same space as the note, and must also be just the right size.

Right	Wrong	Right	Wrong	Right	Wrong
♯o	♯o	♭o	♭o	♮o	♮o

Sharps

Sharps look just like a hashtag sign, with the lines across sloping up.

Notice how the vertical lines are quite long. The 'middle square' is the part that must line up with the note. (See above)

Trace and draw some sharps next to these notes. (Remember, accidentals always go on the LEFT of the note)

Flats

Flats look like a lower case 'b' that is pointy at the bottom.

The round part of the flat must line up with the note. (See above)

Trace and draw some flats here:

Go to **blitzbooks.com** and download some FREE manuscript to practise drawing notes with sharps and flats!

Naturals

These are the trickiest to draw. Imagine drawing a capital 'L' followed by another one upside down. The lines across slope up just a little bit! The middle part of the natural sign should line up with the note (see previous page).

Trace and draw some natural signs here:

Add the correct accidental to these notes. (Remember, the sign goes BEFORE the note!)

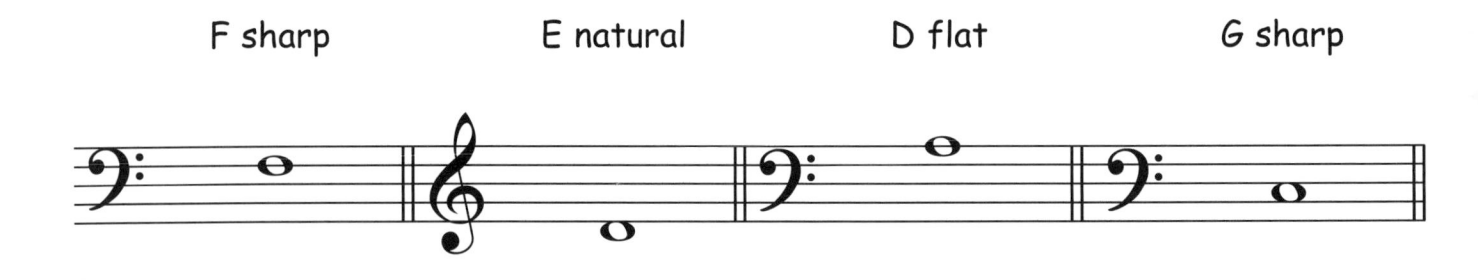

F sharp   E natural   D flat   G sharp

F flat   D sharp   A natural   C flat

G flat   B sharp   G natural   C natural

Accidentals on Leger Lines

Sometimes you are asked to write a note on a leger line (that is, 'above' or 'below' the staff) which also needs an accidental. Take a look at this note:

The sharp does NOT need its own leger line! It just hangs in the air next to the note.

By the way, what note is this? _____

So, here's the order to do things:
1. Draw the leger line or lines.
2. Draw the note.
3. Draw the accidental.

Now try writing 'C sharp below the stave', following the three steps above:

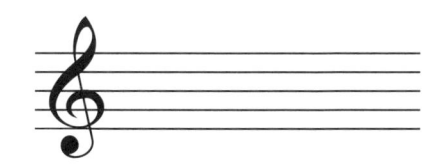

Add the correct accidentals to each of these leger line notes, then name the note!

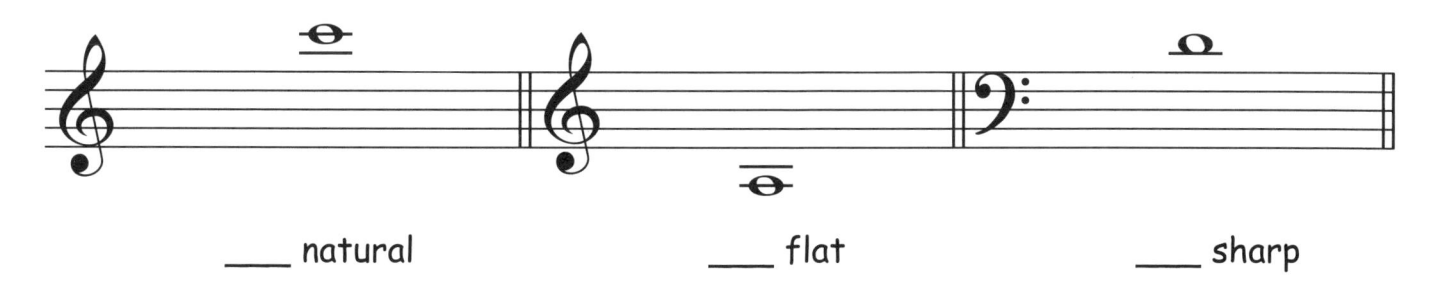

___ natural   ___ flat   ___ sharp

Write these leger line notes with the correct accidental. (Remember the three steps above...)

D flat above the staff

E natural below the staff

C sharp above the staff

B flat below the staff

17

Naming Notes

When naming notes, it is important to write the answer using LETTER NAMES and to use CAPITAL LETTERS as if you are SHOUTING THE ANSWER. (bahaha)

Try naming these notes:

✓ **CHECK:** Capital letters used ☐   Changes of clef noticed ☐

If you are tested on naming notes with accidentals, you have to use WORDS for ♯, ♭ and ♮ signs! Circle the correct answer below:

C♯   C sharp   C flat

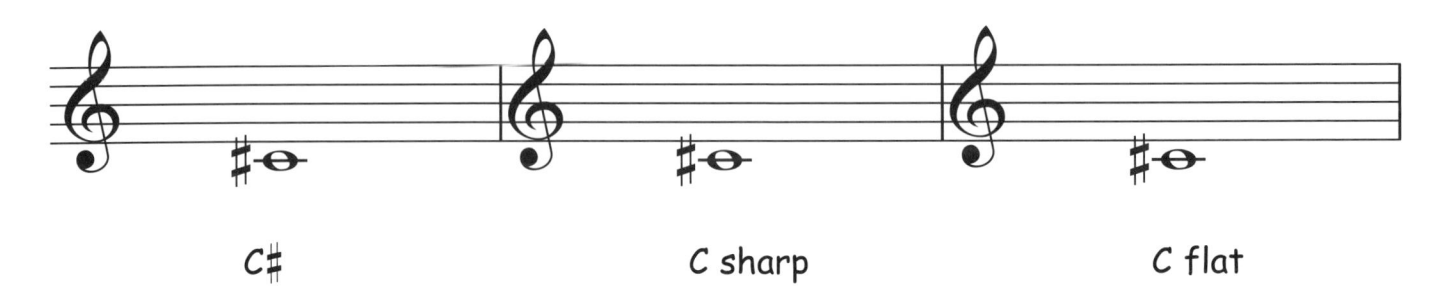

Name these notes. Remember to use CAPITAL LETTERS and use words for ♯, ♭ and ♮.

HOT TIP: These questions deliberately try to trick you by switching from 𝄞 to 𝄢 a lot. Always double-check your work!

Drawing Notes

Sometimes a question involves at least 2 or 3 steps before you reach the correct answer. The important thing is to READ THE QUESTION CAREFULLY.

1. Draw the following note as a dotted minim:

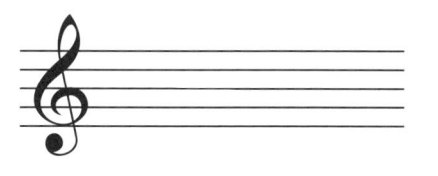

   G sharp on a line

   ★ The G must be written on a _____, not in a space.
   ★ To make it a dotted minim you'll need to add a _____ and a _____ ! (See page 10 for direction of stems and positions of dots)
   ★ You must draw a _____ sign in front of the note.

2. Write the following note as a crotchet:

   See how the question asks for 'B natural', not just 'B'? You MUST draw the natural sign!

   B natural above the staff

   ✓ CHECK: Crotchet ☐   Natural sign ☐   Above the staff ☐

3. Draw the following notes as minims using leger lines. (Hint: Sometimes the question doesn't tell you whether to draw the notes above or below the staff – if this happens, you can choose!)

   C natural   B flat   E   C sharp

   (No natural sign needed here!)

19

Know Your Notes!

1. Write the following notes as semibreves:

   E flat on a line   C below the staff   C sharp above the staff

2. Draw the following notes:

   A flat as a minim in the bass clef   **D sharp** as a crotchet in the treble clef

3. Name these notes. Use words for ♯, ♭ and ♮.

   ....

4. Place the correct clef before these notes:

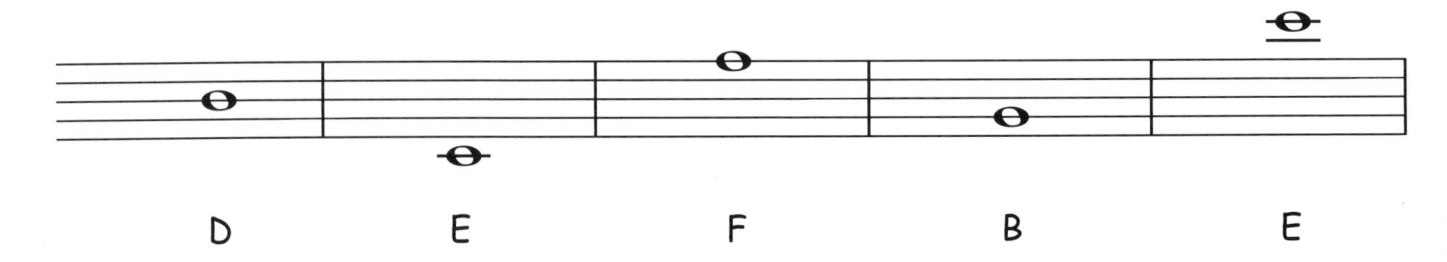

   D   E   F   B   E

5. Add a sign to this note to make it sound one semitone higher:

6. Now find this note on the keyboard diagram on page 14.
   It's a black note... what is the other possible name for it? _____

Yet Another Worksheet on Notes

1. Write each of these notes in three different places using crotchets:

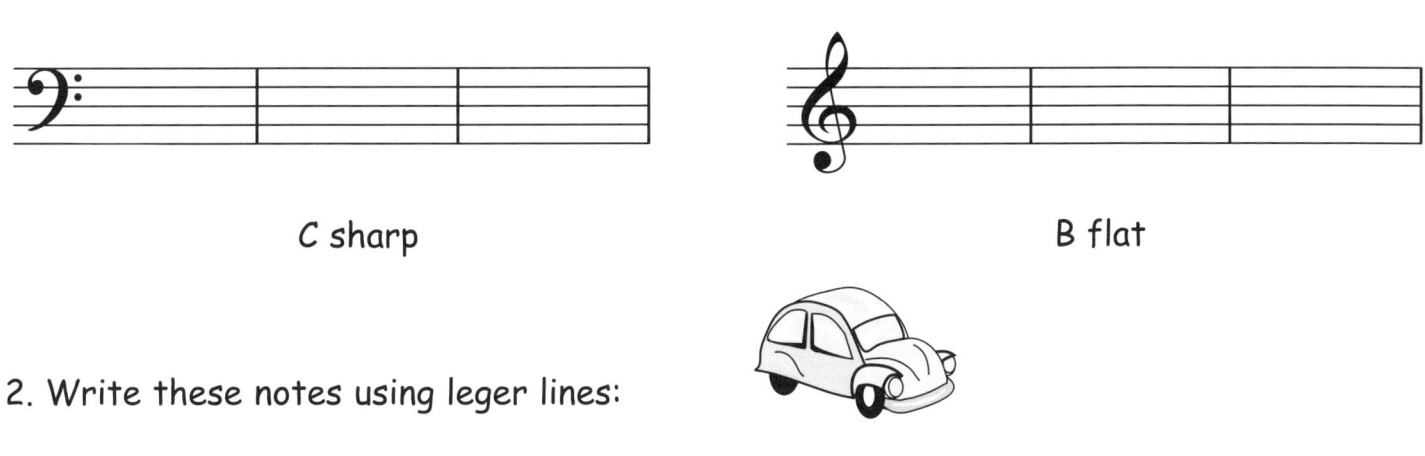

   C sharp   B flat

2. Write these notes using leger lines:

   B sharp   A natural   C sharp   E flat

3. The note one semitone lower than B has two possible names: __ flat or __ sharp.

4. Write these notes using accidentals:

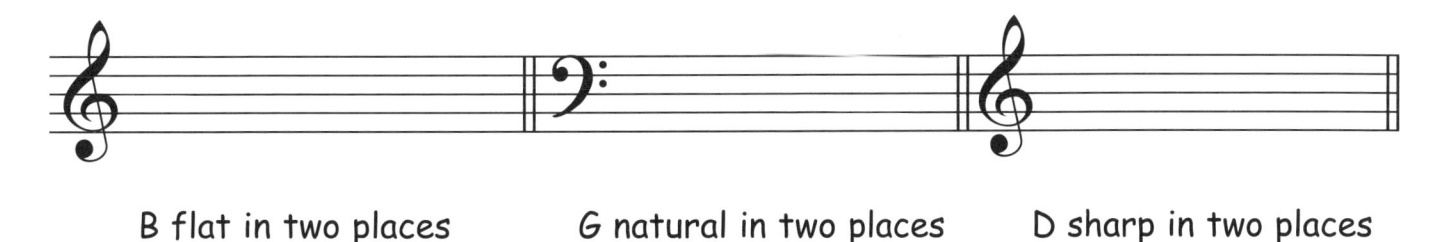

   B flat in two places   G natural in two places   D sharp in two places

5. Draw the following:

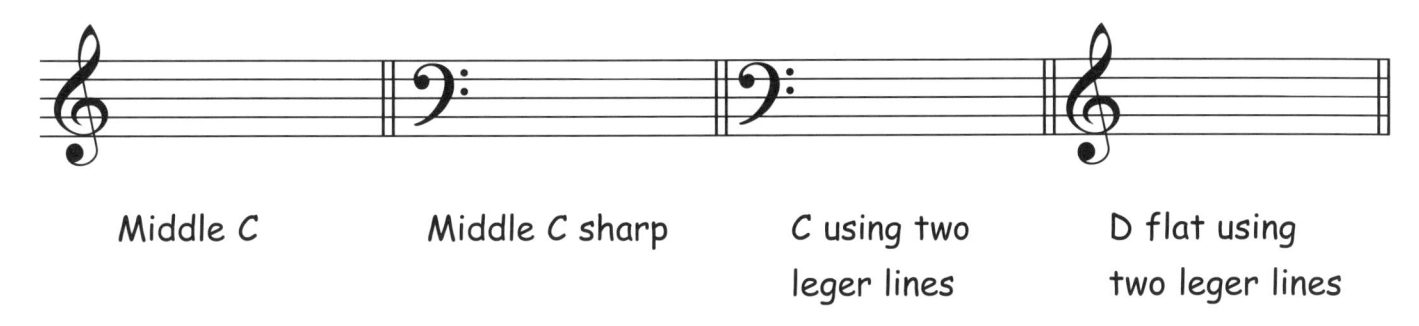

   Middle C   Middle C sharp   C using two   D flat using
                                             leger lines   two leger lines

Tones, Semitones and the Major Scale

★ A **semitone** is the distance between a note and its nearest neighbour. (See page 14)

★ A **tone** is made up of two semitones - just like a circle is made up of two semicircles!

You've probably played some major scales before. They sound similar to each other; they just start on different notes. Major scales sound similar because they are all based on the following pattern:

Tone-Tone-Semitone-Tone-Tone-Tone-Semitone (T-T-S-T-T-T-S)

Let's look at the C major scale:

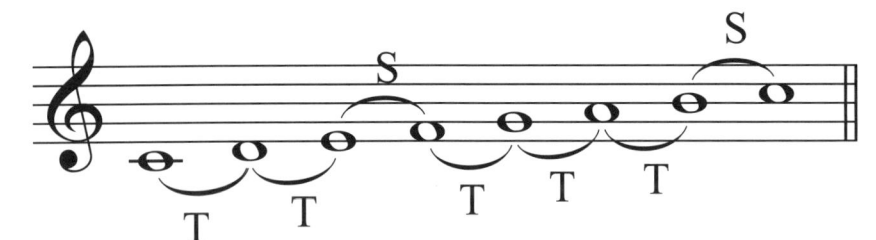

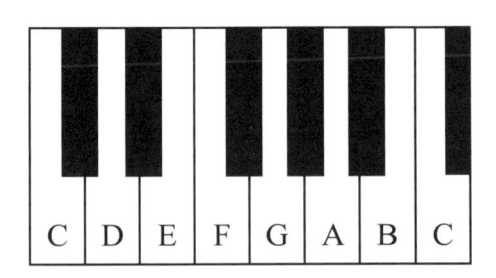

> It just so happens that C major does not need any sharps or flats to make the pattern T-T-S-T-T-T-S. This is why **C major has NO SHARPS OR FLATS**.

How about G major:

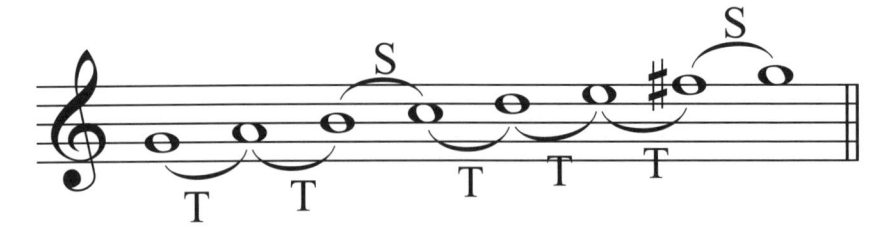

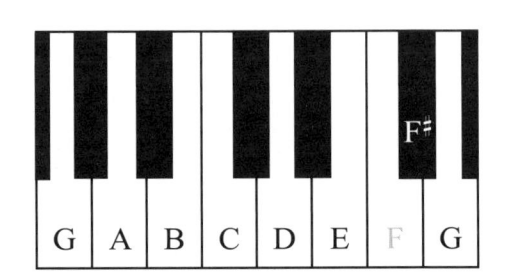

> E to F is only a semitone. We need the F♯ to make a tone in the right spot. This is why **G major has an F SHARP**.

And now for the F major scale:

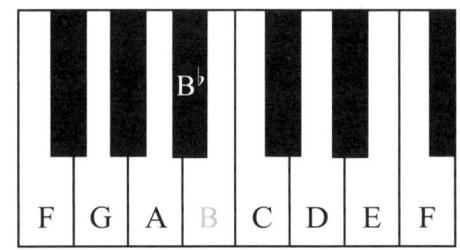

A to B is a tone, so we need the B♭ to make a semitone in the right spot. This is why **F major has a B FLAT**.

If you know which sharps or flats are in a scale, then you know its **KEY SIGNATURE**. A key signature shows which scale a piece of music is based on.

There are no sharps or flats in a C major scale. The **key signature** has nothing in it!

There is an F sharp in the scale of G major, so the **key signature** of G major is F sharp.

There is a B flat in the scale of F major, so the **key signature** of F major is B flat.

Practice drawing the G and F major key signatures in treble and bass. They must look exactly right!

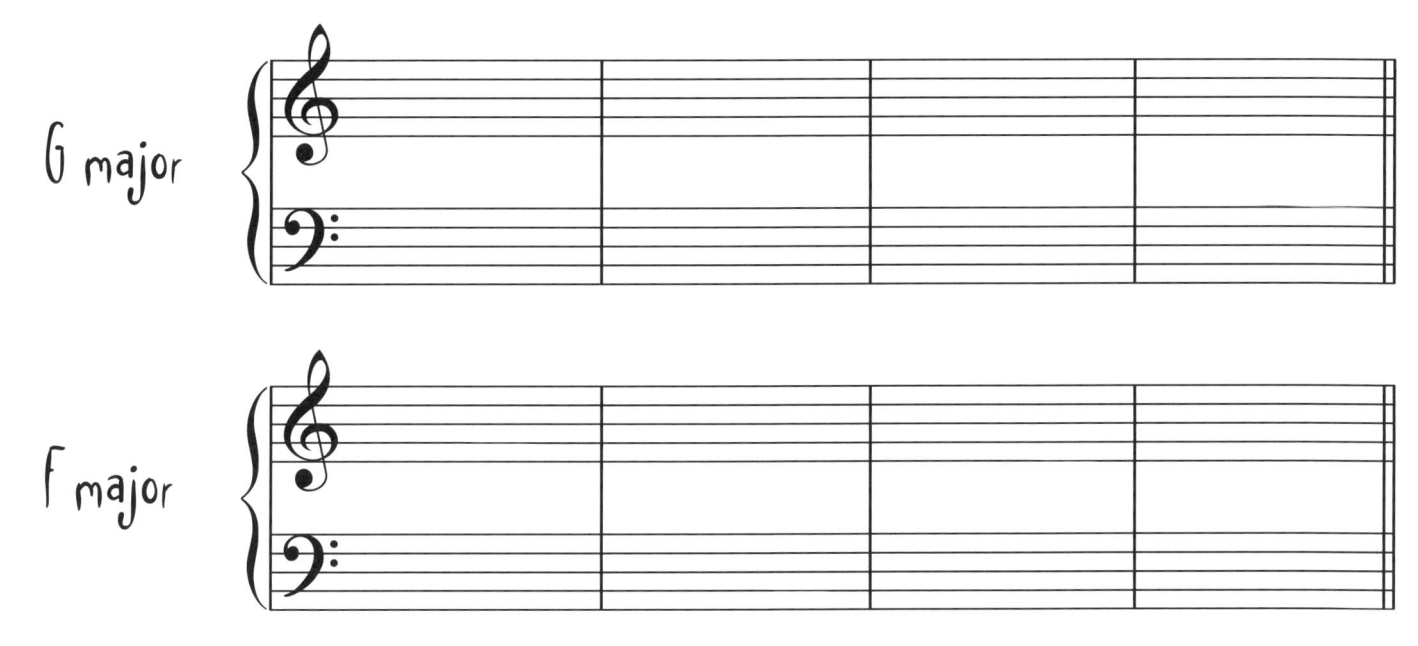

G major

F major

Scale Degree Numbers

Each note in the scale has a number. The **lowest** note is always no. 1.

Finish writing the scale degree numbers under this C major scale.

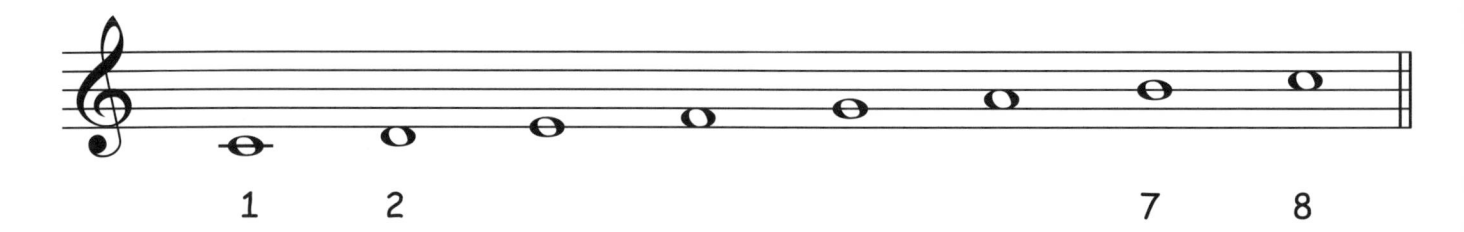

1   2   7   8

Now write the rest of the numbers under this G major scale:

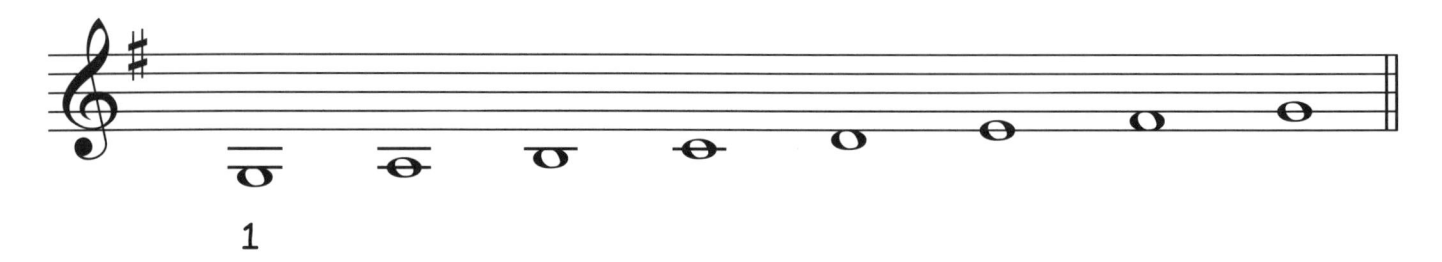

1

As you can see, the numbers are the same, but the notes are different!

Here's an F major scale that's going DOWN. Finish writing in the scale degree numbers:

2   1

See how the numbers start at the bottom? The lowest note is no. 1!

Quick Quiz:

What is the name of note no. 1 in C major? ____

What is the name of note no. 1 in F major? ____

What is the name of note no. 1 in G major? ____

} Do you notice a bit of a pattern here???

24

Marking Semitones in Scales

Often you are asked to 'mark the semitones' in a scale. This means to put a curved line called a 'slur' between the notes that are a semitone apart.

The best way to remember where the semitones live is by which **scale degree numbers** they fall between. Write the scale degree numbers under this F major scale:

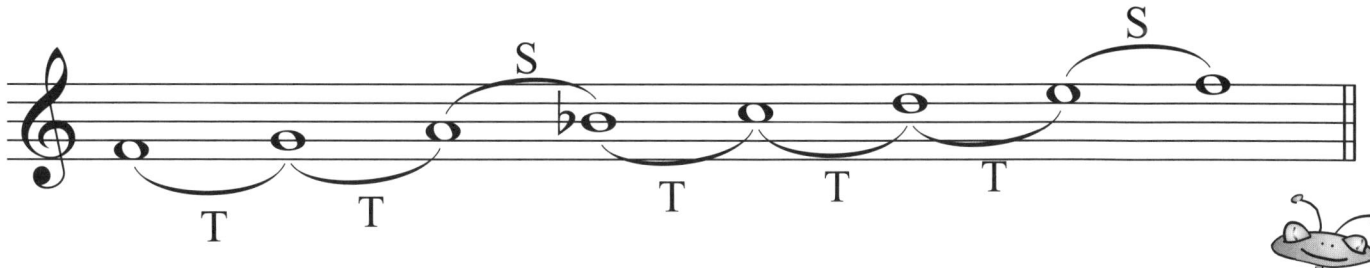

Between which numbers are the semitones? ____ - ____ and ____ - ____

Let's check this with a scale that's going down. Write the numbers under the scale below, starting from the BOTTOM note - the lowest note is number 1!

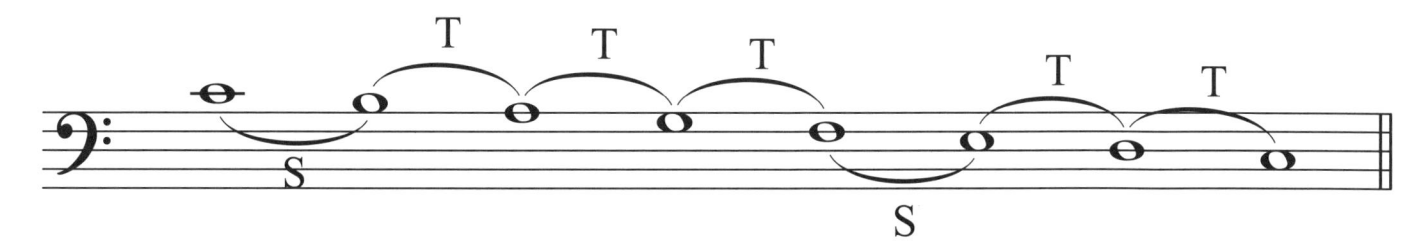

Between which numbers are the semitones? ____ - ____ and ____ - ____

So when we mark the semitones in a scale, we simply put a slur between scale degrees 3-4 and 7-8!

HOT TIP: Semitones in major scales ALWAYS occur between scale degrees 3-4 and 7-8. You may find this easier to remember than TTSTTTS... whatever works for you!

Try marking the semitones in this scale:

Did you start from the lowest note? Well done!

Let's Get the Semitones Right

Handy Hints:

★ If the stems are going UP, put the slur **under**, e.g.

★ If the stems are going DOWN, put the slur **over**, e.g.

★ If one is up and one is down, you can **choose**, e.g.   or   !

★ IMPORTANT: Look carefully at the slurs above... see how they do not actually touch the notes!

Quick revision: Where do the semitones fall in a major scale? Between ___-___ and ___-___!

Mark the semitones in these scales with a slur:

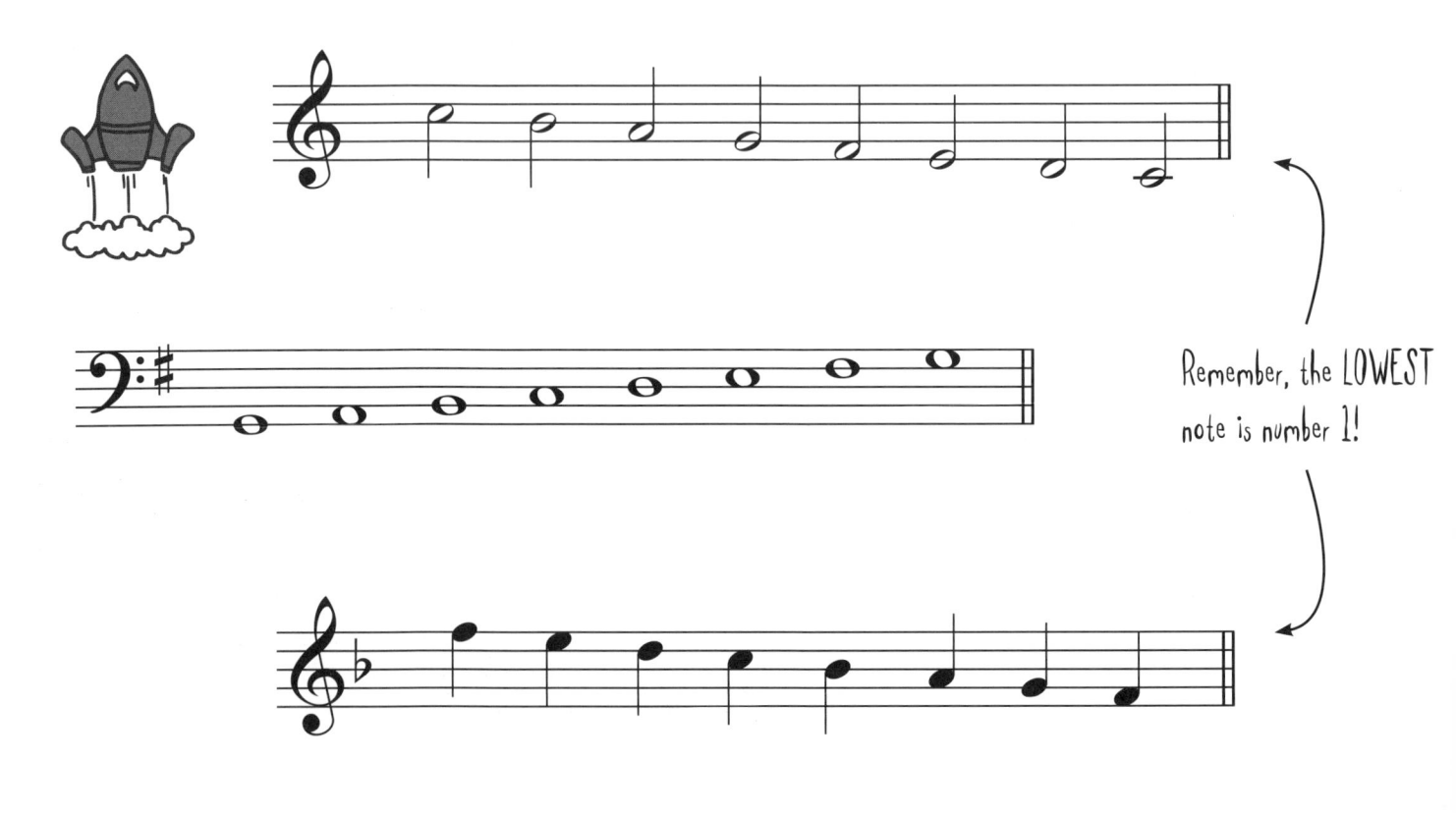

Remember, the LOWEST note is number 1!

Marking Tones in Scales

If we practise this enough it becomes incredibly easy.

Just for fun, mark the semitones in this scale with **red slurs**:

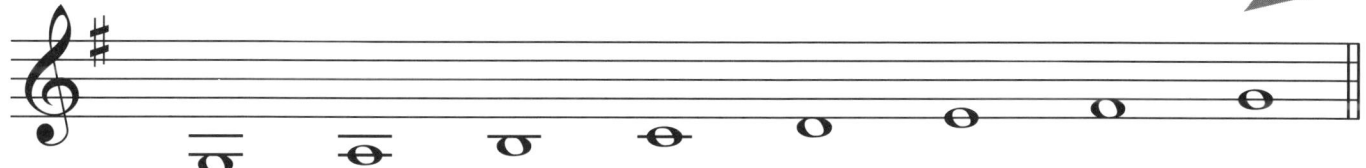

Let's mark the tones as well, but with **blue slurs**. You should now have a slur between every note!

How many semitones are in the scale? _____   How many tones? _____

So, if you are asked to mark only the **tones** in a scale, simply put a slur from one note to the next, but leave out 3-4 and 7-8. They are not tones, they are _____!

Mark the tones in the following scales:

Things to Check:

★ Do you have 5 tones marked in each scale?   Yes/No

★ Did you remember the lowest note is number 1? Yes/No

Tiny Test

Total: /28

1. Mark each of these pairs of notes with an 'S' for semitone or a 'T' for tone. Use the diagram on page 14 to help you! /5

2. Here is a G major scale all mixed up. Write in the scale degree numbers. /7

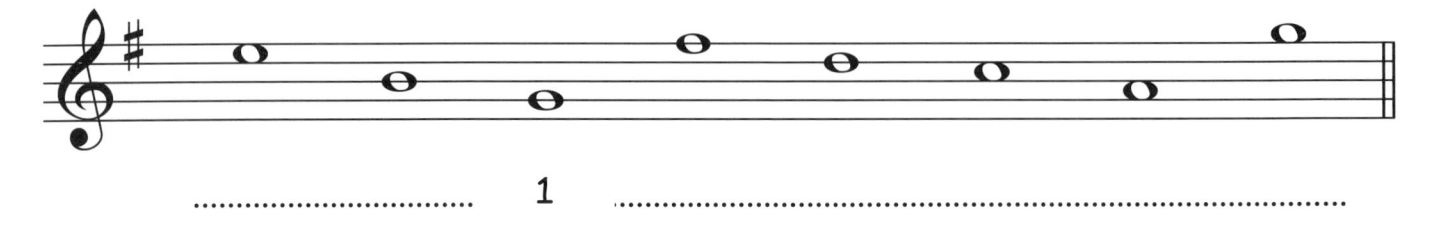

.... 1 ....

3. Write the following key signatures. (Watch out for the clef changes!) /4

F major   G major   F major   G major

4. Add the correct key signature to this F major scale. Then mark the tones. /6

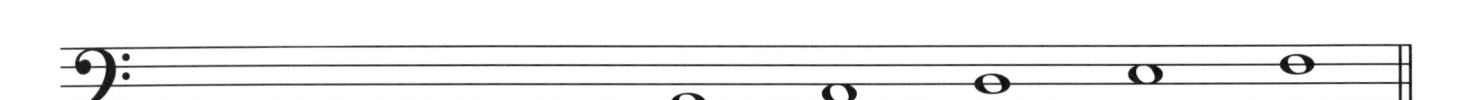

5. Write the correct notes for these F major scale degree numbers. Check the clef. (Warning: accidental required for one of the notes!) /6

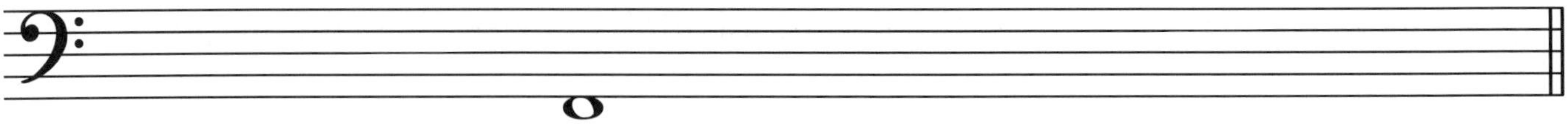

6   4   1   5   7   3   2

Key Signatures vs Accidentals

Scales can be written two ways:

1. With the key signature at the beginning:

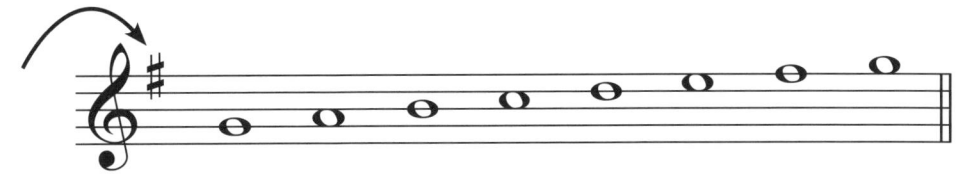

OR...

2. With an accidental instead of the key signature:

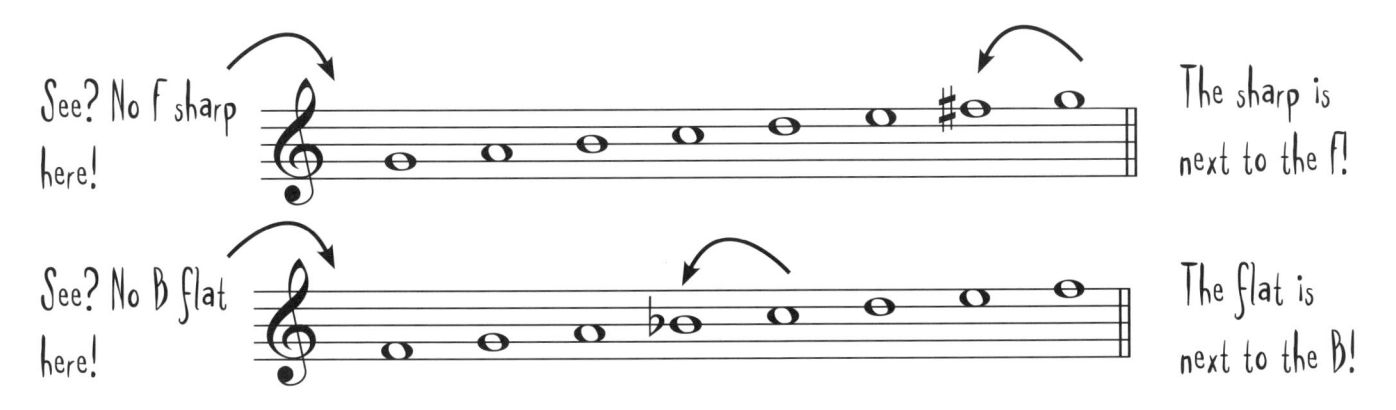

See? No F sharp here! ... The sharp is next to the F!

See? No B flat here! ... The flat is next to the B!

HOT TIP: Scales are written EITHER with a key signature at the beginning OR with an accidental in the right place — never with both!

These scales don't have key signatures, they need accidentals. You'll need to work out which scales they are by looking at the first and last notes! (Hint: It's always C, G or F major!)

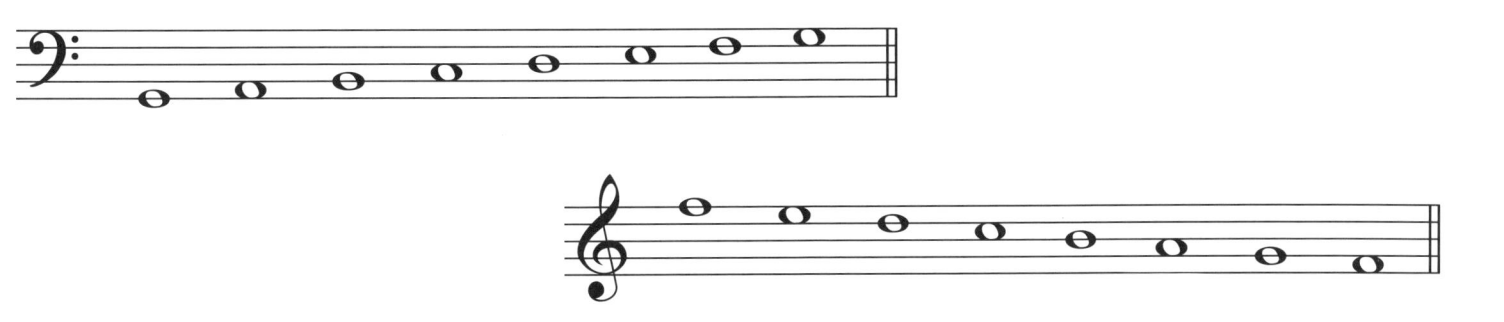

Tricky one now... add the correct **clef** and **accidental** to make this an F major scale. (oooaaahh)

Awesome Accidentals

Add accidentals to make the following scales correct, then add a double bar line:

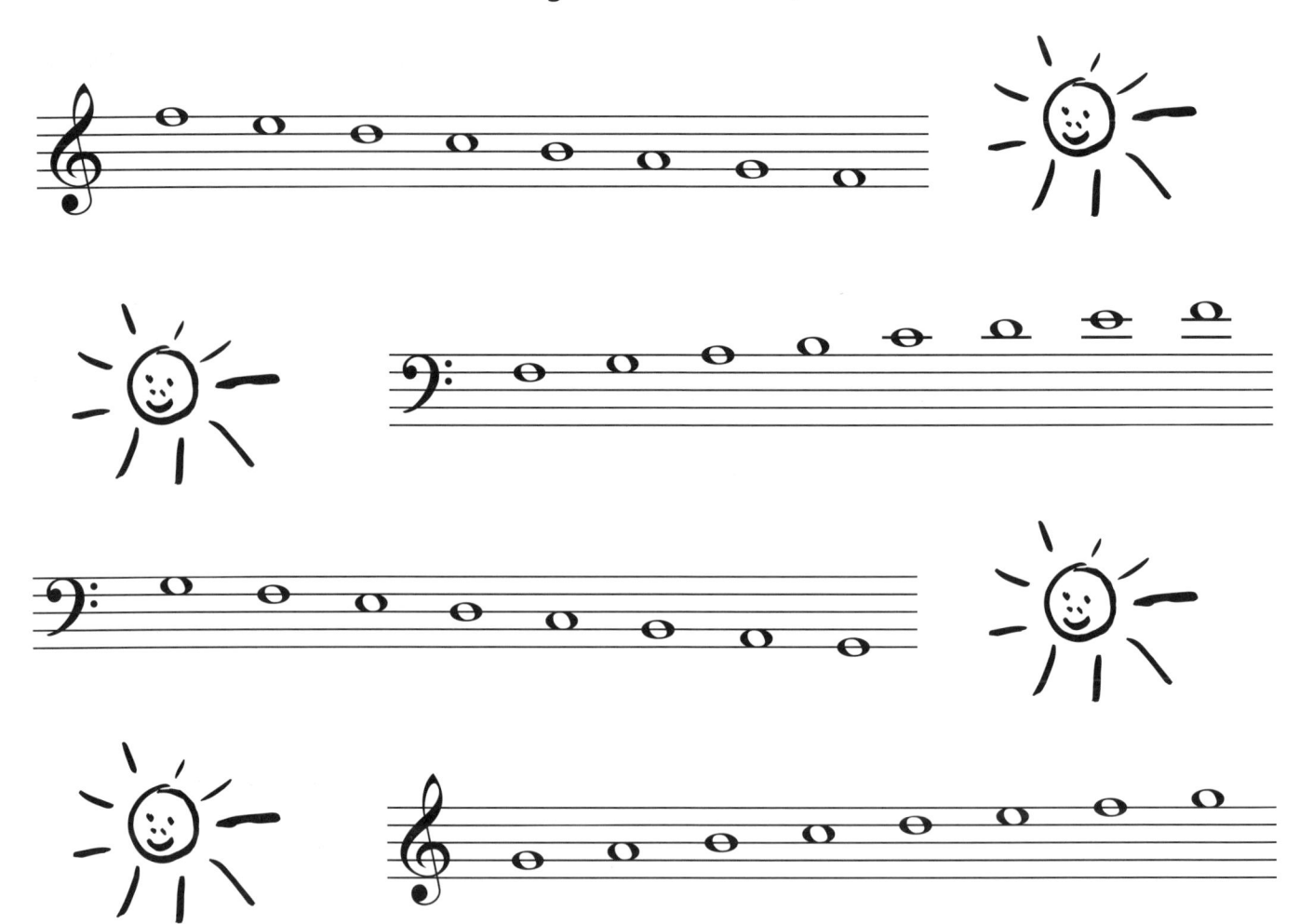

Add a clef and accidental to make this into a G major scale:

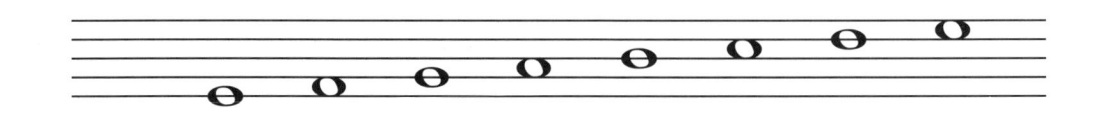

Have you put your accidentals BEFORE the notes?

Quick Quiz:

What's the difference between an accidental and a key signature? _____

_____

Which one of them goes at the beginning of the staff? _____

Writing Scales

The trick to writing scales is to be able to **follow instructions**.

You must read the question extremely carefully, and there are lots of different ways it might be worded. Try this one:

Write the scale of G major:

★ use a key signature

★ use minims

★ write one octave going down (also known as 'descending')

★ mark the semitones

★ complete the scale with a double bar line

Handy Hints:

★ Space the notes out evenly - try putting your pinky (5th) finger between each note.

★ Do NOT assume the scale is to be written in the treble. The question may ask for treble or bass; in fact very often the clef is already given. Always check the clef!

★ Many people fall into the trap of marking the semitones instead of the tones, or the other way around. Put a circle around the word 'tones' or 'semitones' so you don't accidentally do the wrong thing!

★ Always double check whether you've been asked to use **accidentals** or a **key signature**.

★ Go back and tick off each instruction after checking you have done it.

Let's Write Scales

1. Write the scale of F major:
   - use accidentals - NOT the key signature
   - use semibreves
   - write one octave descending
   - mark the tones
   - finish with a double bar line

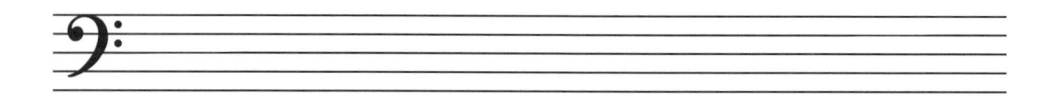

2. Write the key signature of G major. Now write that scale:
   - write one octave going up (also known as 'ascending')
   - use crotchets
   - mark each semitone with a slur
   - complete the scale with a double bar line

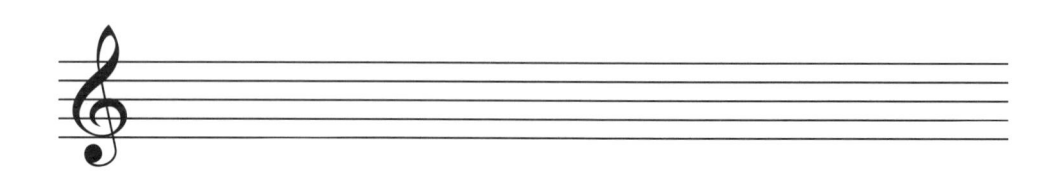

3. Write the scale of C major:
   - use the bass clef
   - write one octave ascending
   - use minims
   - mark the tones

Quick Revision: The semitones in a major scale fall between __-__ and __-__!

More Scales

1. Add the correct clef and key signature to make this the scale of G major:

2. Now make the notes in the scale above into minims and mark the semitones.

3. Write the scale of C major:

    * use accidentals (hint: this is a trick)
    * use crotchets
    * write one octave ascending
    * mark each tone with a slur
    * complete the scale with a double bar line

Did you see the clef?

4. Name these scales:

Scale: _____

Scale: _____

Scale Trivia

1. Finish this descending (which means 'going down') scale using crotchets. Then add the necessary clef and key signature to make it an F major scale.

2. Where do the semitones fall in major scales? Between ___-___ and ___-___ . Now mark them in the scale above!

3. Circle the correct G major key signature. (It must be correct in both treble AND bass!)

4. Accidentals are always written:

   A. before the note   B. after the note   C. on top of the note

5. When marking tones or semitones in a scale, always start from:

   A. the highest note   B. the lowest note   C. the beginning

6. Name the scales that have the following key signatures:

Timed Test

Time:

Time yourself doing this page. Do it as fast as you can, then record your finishing time above. But... guess what? Your teacher will **ADD ON 10 SECONDS** for every mistake you make! It's fun to go fast, but it's more important to be **accurate**. Start the clock!

1. In every major scale there are ___ semitones and ___ tones.

2. Name this key signature: _____

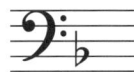

3. Semitones fall between scale degrees ___ - ___ and ___ - ___ .

4. Finish this ascending scale using minims. Then add the correct accidental!

5. Mark the tones in the scale above.

6. 𝅗𝅥 + 𝅗𝅥. + 𝅘𝅥 + 𝅘𝅥𝅮𝅘𝅥𝅮 + 𝄽 = ___ beats.

7. Write these notes as crotchets using leger lines:

   C natural   B sharp   E natural   C flat

STOP THE CLOCK - FILL IN YOUR TIME AT THE TOP!

After marking this with your teacher, tick one of the following:

☐ I made no mistakes! I keep my time of _____ !

☐ I made ___ mistakes. My new time is _____ .

Naming the Key of a Melody

Melodies are always based on a certain scale - this means they are in a certain 'key'. There are two clues to look for when working out the key of a melody.

1. The key signature (for Grade 1 only C, G or F major);

2. The last note - melodies usually end on scale degree no. 1 - the 'tonic'.

Here is a melody in G major:

Key signature of G major

Melody ends on a G (scale degree no.1)

Here is another melody:

The key signature contains a B flat. Which scale has this key signature? _____

What is the last note of the melody? ____ (make sure you check the clef)

So this melody is in the key of _____ .

Name the key of these short melodies. Remember your two clues, and check the clef!

Key: _____

Key: _____

Key: _____

Scale Degree Numbers in Melodies

Writing scale degrees under a melody is just like writing them under a scale, except that the notes are 'out of order'. A tune can start on any degree of the scale.

Write in the missing scale degrees for this famous tune in G major:

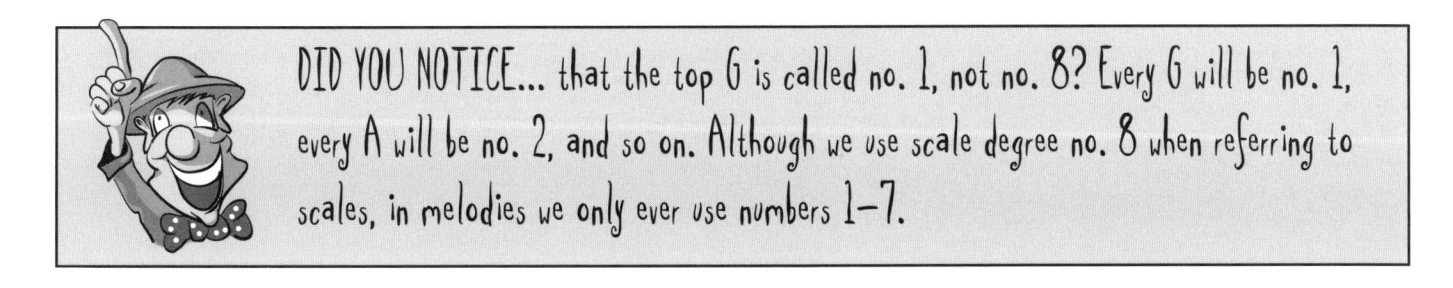

5 1 2 .... 7 1 1 ....

DID YOU NOTICE... that the top G is called no. 1, not no. 8? Every G will be no. 1, every A will be no. 2, and so on. Although we use scale degree no. 8 when referring to scales, in melodies we only ever use numbers 1-7.

Finish writing the scale degree numbers under these melodies. Use numbers 1-7 only!

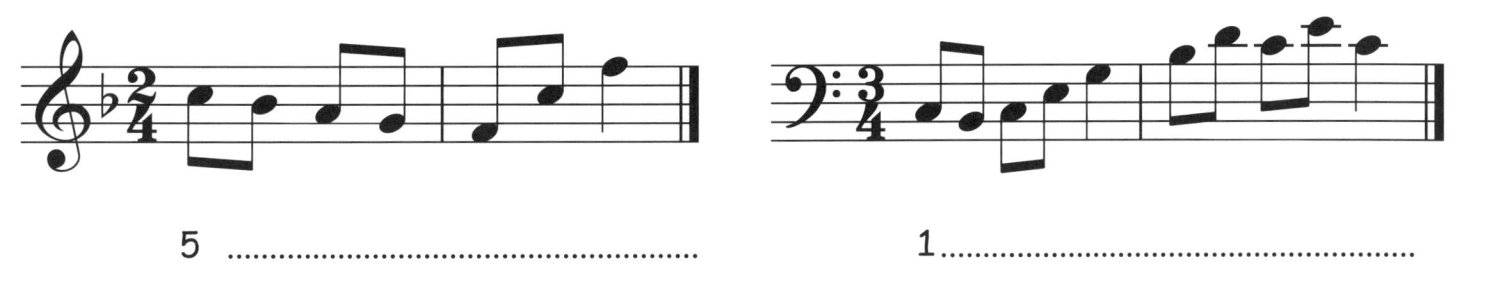

5 ....   1 ....

In the melodies below, work out which note is no. 1, then fill in all the scale degree numbers. To do this you must work out the **KEY** first (which we've just been practising!) and then double check the **CLEF**.

Key: _____

....

Key: _____

....

37

Helpful Hints for Scale Degrees

★ If the notes go UP, count 1, 2, 3 etc.

★ If the notes go DOWN, count backwards: 1(8), 7, 6 etc.

★ Do **NOT** assume the melody will start on scale degree no. 1 - it often doesn't!

★ Melodies usually end on scale degree no. 1. **Beware** of ending on a different number... you might have misread the key or the clef!

Check List: Correct Key ☐   Clef ☐   Only numbers 1-7 used ☐

1.

2.

3.

4.

Scales 'n' Stuff

1. Circle the correct F major key signature. (It must be correct in both treble AND bass!)

2. Write the scale degree numbers under the notes of this melody.

3. Here's a bit of a tricky question: in the melody above, mark all the semitones with a slur. (Hint: you'll need to look for 3-4, 4-3, 7-1 and 1-7!)

4. What is the other name for a semibreve rest? _____

5. Write these notes as dotted minims using leger lines:

B flat   D natural   A sharp   C flat

Go to **blitzbooks.com** for heaps of fantastic worksheets, and for great games such as Beat Bingo, all completely FREE!

Intervals

★ An interval is the distance between two notes.

★ The bottom note is known as the 'tonic' note - scale degree no. 1.

An interval where both notes are the same pitch is called a 'unison' (it is never called a '1st'). To name an interval, simply count up from the bottom note. Fill in the missing names:

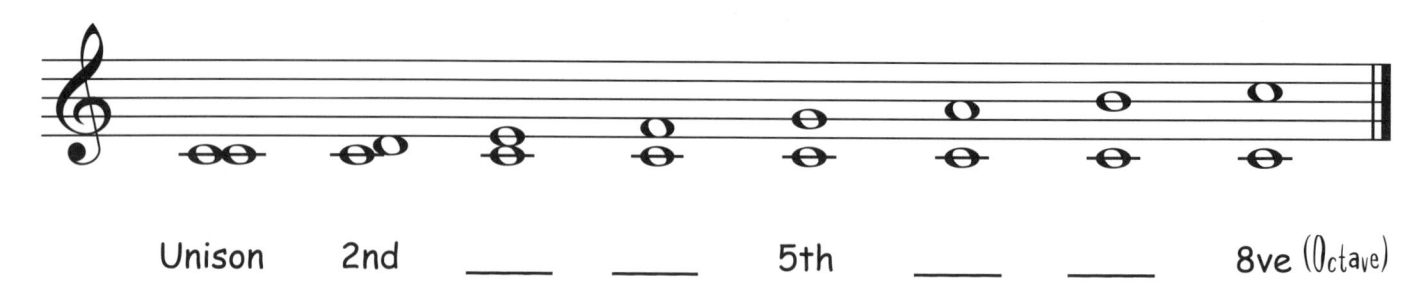

Unison   2nd   ____   ____   5th   ____   ____   8ve (Octave)

Name these intervals above the tonic of F. Remember, the bottom note counts as no. 1!

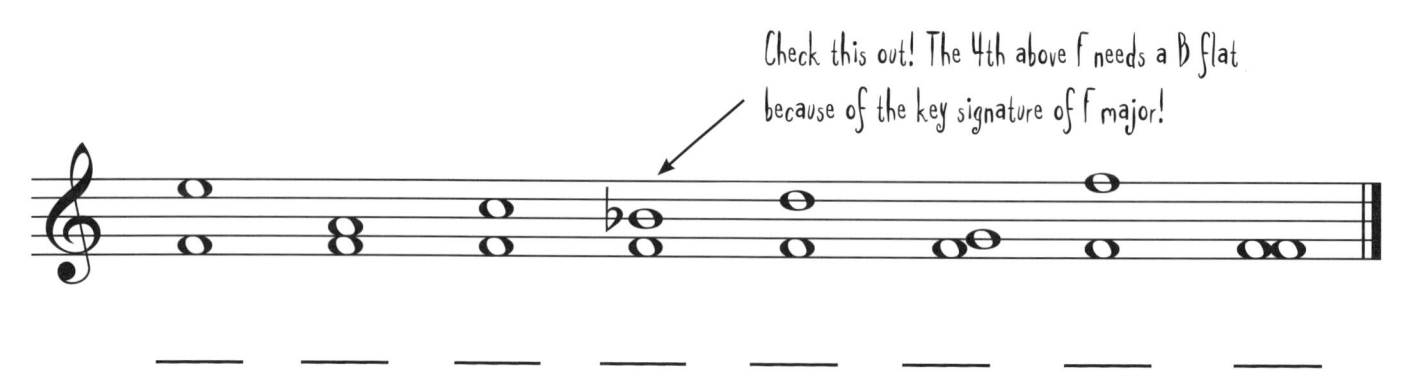

Check this out! The 4th above F needs a B flat because of the key signature of F major!

____ ____ ____ ____ ____ ____ ____

Name these intervals above the tonic of G. Same deal as before... bottom note is no. 1!

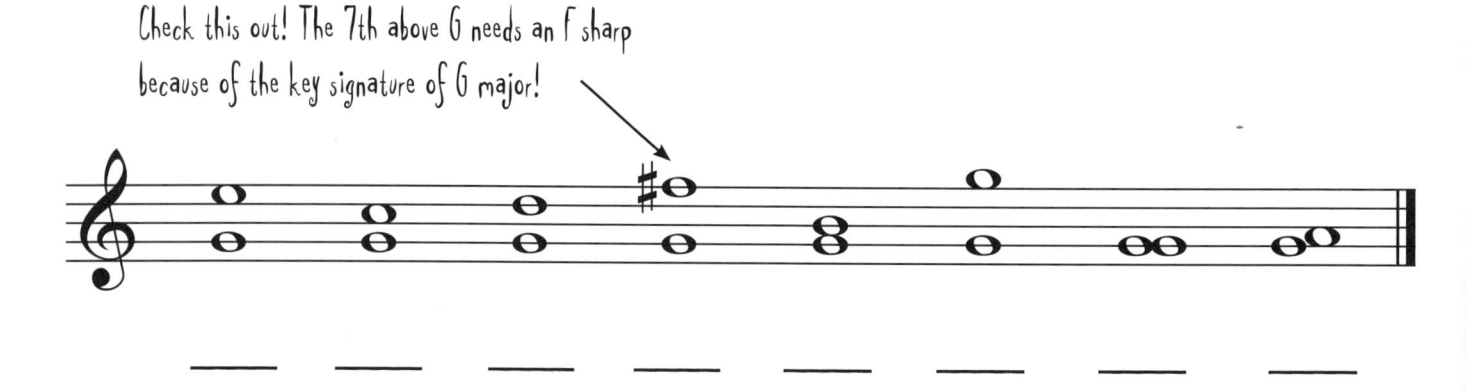

Check this out! The 7th above G needs an F sharp because of the key signature of G major!

____ ____ ____ ____ ____ ____ ____

Q: Which two intervals require accidentals? A: The 4th above ___ and the 7th above ___ !!!!

Writing Intervals is Easy

Sometimes you are asked to draw an interval above a certain tonic note. The tonic note shows you which scale the interval comes from.

If the tonic is C, that means C major, which has no sharps or flats. You don't need to worry about any accidentals for intervals in C major. (Phew!)

Write these intervals above C. (Ok, the unison won't be 'above'! It should be so close that it touches the tonic.)

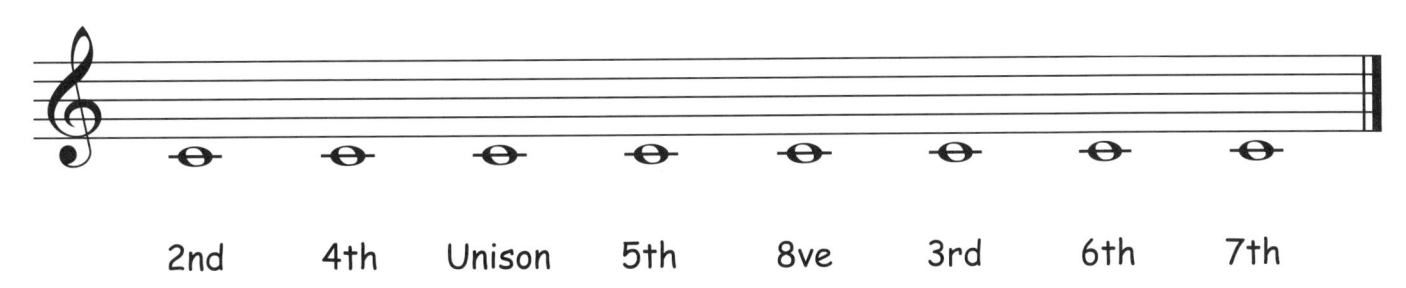

      2nd   4th   Unison   5th   8ve   3rd   6th   7th

Make sure your '2nd' is to the side like this _____ not this _____ !

If the tonic note is G, that means ___ major, which has an F sharp. There's just one interval which will need an accidental... (hint: see previous page!)

Write these intervals above G:

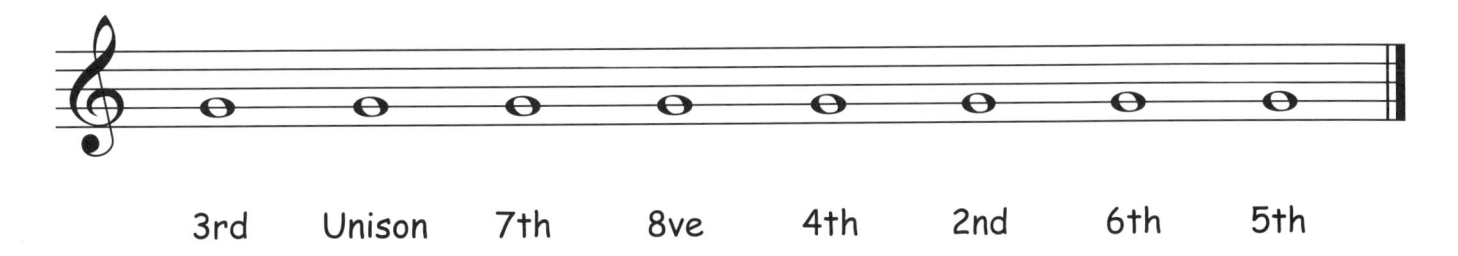

      3rd   Unison   7th   8ve   4th   2nd   6th   5th

If the tonic note is F, that means ___ major, which has a ___ _____. Again, there's only one interval which will need an accidental...

Now write these intervals above F:

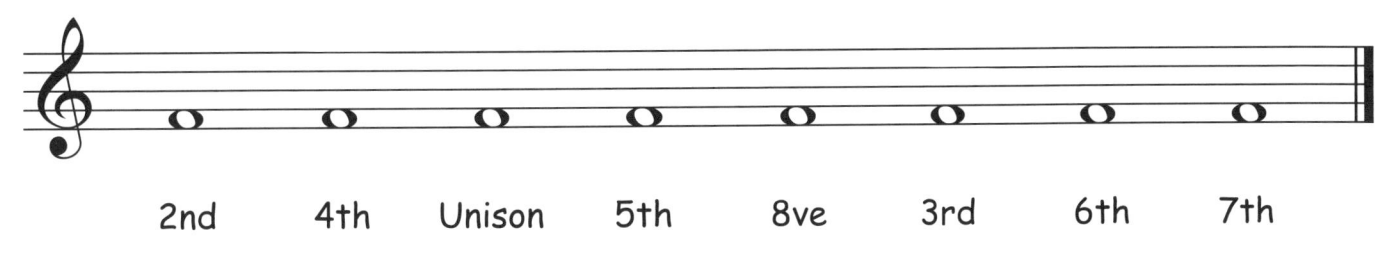

      2nd   4th   Unison   5th   8ve   3rd   6th   7th

Intervals on Leger Lines

If the given tonic note is very high, you will need to use leger lines to draw your intervals. Don't be tempted to write intervals underneath - they must always go ABOVE!

1. Trace these intervals with leger lines, then name each interval. (Remember, trace the leger lines first, then the note.)

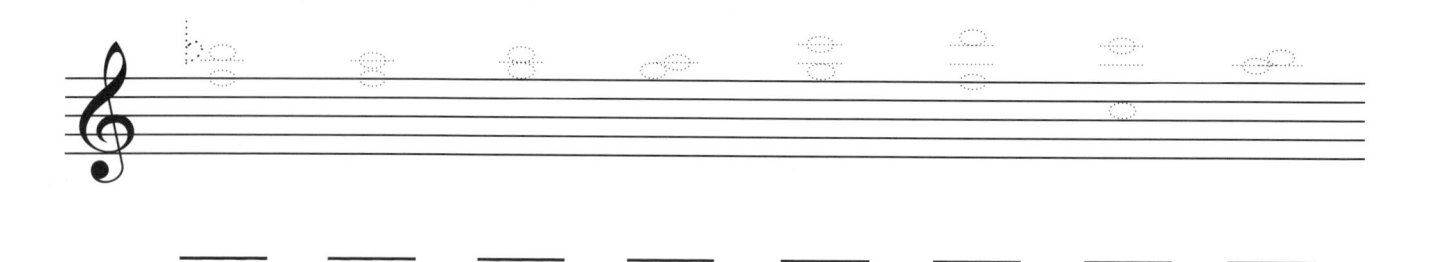

2. Write the following intervals above the given tonic: (yes, you'll have to use leger lines)

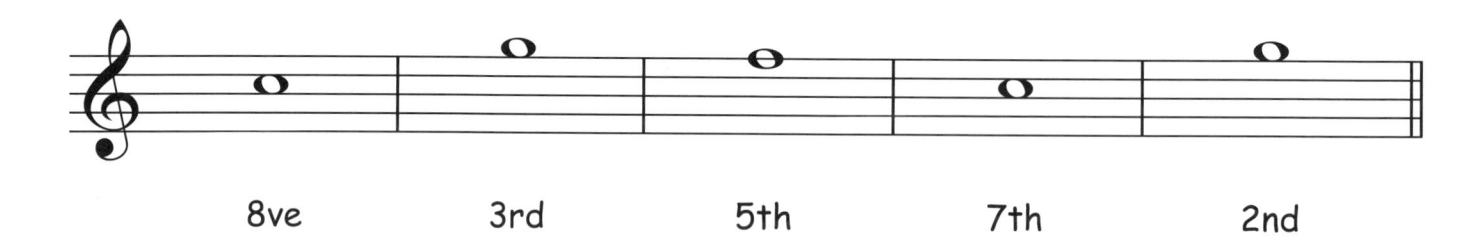

8ve   3rd   5th   7th   2nd

3. Name these intervals by number only (see 'Hot Tip' below):

HOT TIP: When we get to Grade 2, naming intervals gets more complicated, but for now we name them 'by number only'. It does not mean you should leave off the endings of the numbers! Make sure you write your answers using ordinal numbers e.g. 4th, 5th, etc. Also, the intervals we study are 'diatonic' intervals, meaning part of the same scale or key!

Revision of Heaps of Things

1. Write the scale degrees under the notes of these melodies. (Hint: work out the key first!)

....

....

2. There are 5 mistakes in the following scale. Can you circle them?

3. Write these intervals above the given tonic:

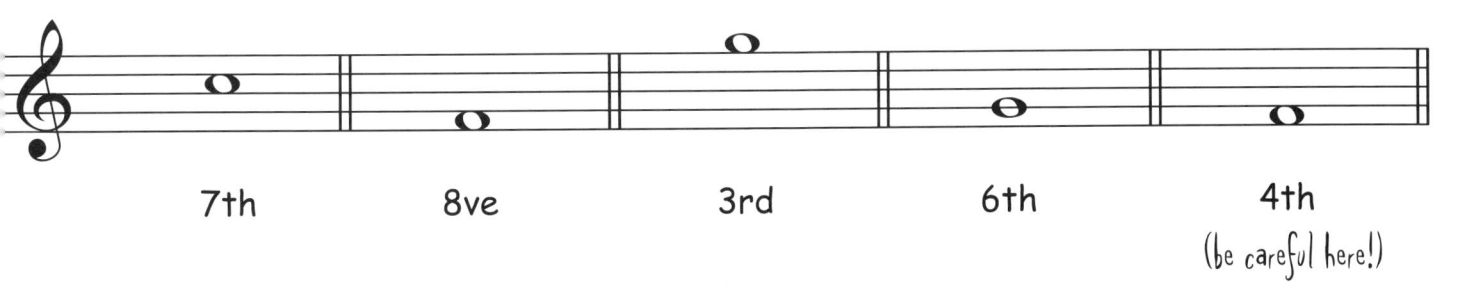

   7th   8ve   3rd   6th   4th
   (be careful here!)

4. Write the following notes as minims:

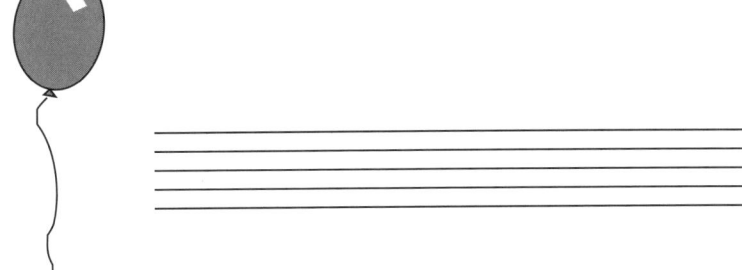

C sharp above the staff in the treble   C natural below the staff in the bass

43

Tonic Triads

★ A 'chord' is two or more notes sounding together.

★ A 'triad' is a chord made up of 3 notes.

★ A 'tonic triad' is a triad built on the tonic - scale degree no. 1. The other two notes are scale degrees 3 and 5.

★ They stack on top of each other and look sort of like a set of traffic lights! (This is also called 'root position'.)

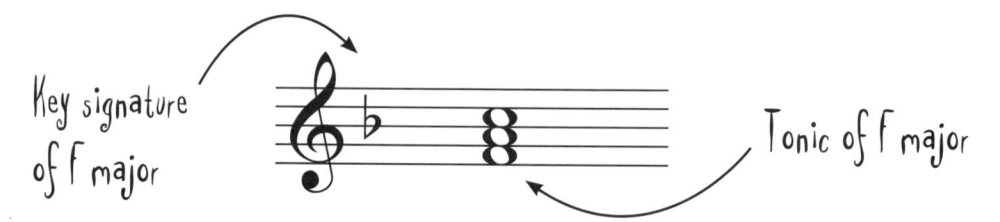

Key signature of F major — Tonic of F major

The above chord is the tonic triad of which key? _____

Try drawing the tonic triad of G major and C major. Use the correct key signature!

G major   C major

Sometimes you'll need leger lines for your tonic triads. It's important to draw these neatly and correctly, so that the notes stack on top of each other properly.

Circle the best-written tonic triads of the following (some of these are rather awful):

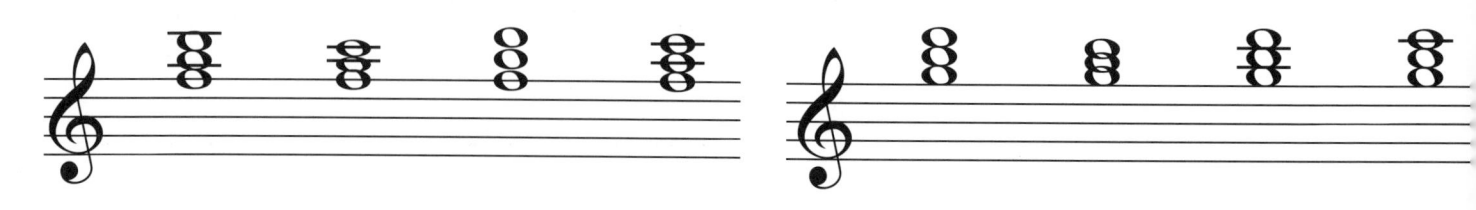

F major   G major

Tonic Triad Practice

1. Trace and draw some tonic triads with leger lines:

2. Complete these tonic triads above the given note, then insert the correct key signature (watch out for clef changes):

    F major   C major   G major   C major   G major

3. Write these tonic triads. Use a key signature.

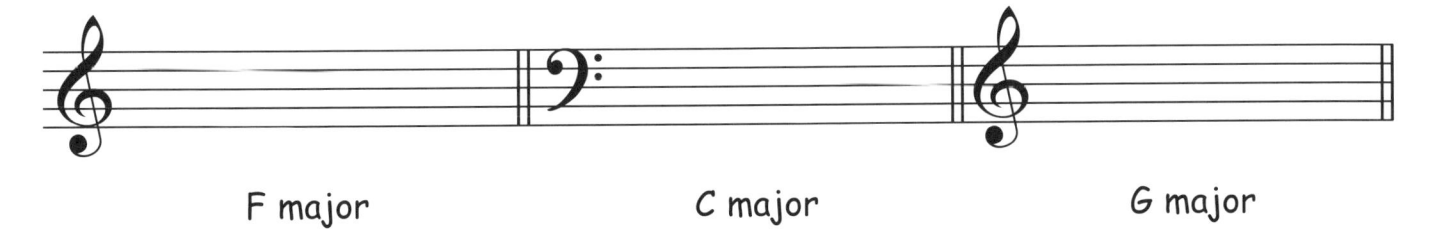

    F major   C major   G major

4. Name these tonic triads.

_____   _____   _____   _____   _____

Did you know... bass clef triads are not tested in the exam, but it's good to do them anyway, don't you think?

Very Important Revision Test

1. Write an F major scale:

   ★ use the bass clef
   ★ use a key signature - not accidentals
   ★ use crotchets
   ★ write one octave ascending
   ★ mark the semitones with slurs
   ★ complete the scale with a double bar line

2. Name these notes. Use words for ♯, ♭ and ♮.

   ....

3. Add the correct cleft and accidentals to these notes:

   G sharp   B natural   D sharp   B flat

4. Write a treble note with the same letter name as each of these bass notes:

5. Name the capital of France _____ (ok this won't really be tested in the exam)   /1

6. Add the correct clef and accidental to make this a G major scale: /2

7. Mark the tones in the above scale.   /5

8. Fill in the missing information in this table. (See page 3 if you need to!)   /14

Note/Rest	Name	Number of Beats
♪		half
	crotchet	
♫	2 quavers	
	_____ rest	2
𝄽		
		4
		whole bar
	minim	

9. Write a 7th above each of these tonic notes. Use accidentals where necessary.   /6

Total: /50

47

Time and Rhythm

First of all, go back to page 3 and revise the values of all the different types of notes and rests. Then try clapping this rhythm through with your teacher:

'Time signature': tells us how many beats per bar

'Bar line': divides the music into equal sections

'Bar': each bar has the same number of beats

'Double bar line': shows us it is the end of the piece

Time Signatures

A time signature gives us information about the rhythm of a piece. The top number tells us the **number** of beats, and the bottom number tells us what kind of beats.

In Grade 1 we study the time signatures $\frac{2}{4}$, $\frac{3}{4}$ and $\frac{4}{4}$, all of which have a '4' on the bottom, meaning 'crotchet' beats.

We also study the time signature **C**, meaning Common Time. It's the same as $\frac{4}{4}$, which is the most common time signature of all!

Time signature	Meaning	Formal Definition
$\frac{2}{4}$	Two crotchet beats per bar	Simple **Duple** time
$\frac{3}{4}$	___ crotchet beats per bar	Simple **Triple** time
$\frac{4}{4}$	___ crotchet beats per bar	Simple **Quadruple** time
C	___ crotchet beats per bar	Simple **Quadruple** time

When you write time signatures, the top and bottom numbers should each take up two spaces within the stave, like this $\frac{2}{4}$ not like this $\frac{2}{4}$!

Insert the correct time signature for each of these rhythms.

Accents

The first beat of a bar is always the **strongest** (S), no matter what the time signature. In $\frac{2}{4}$ and $\frac{3}{4}$, the other beats are **weak** (w).

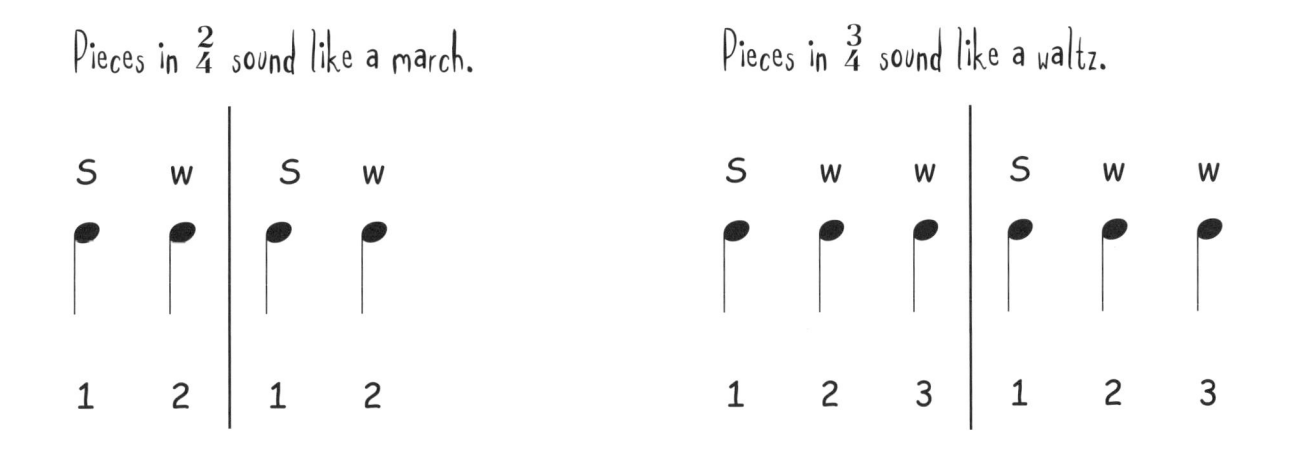

Pieces in $\frac{2}{4}$ sound like a march.

Pieces in $\frac{3}{4}$ sound like a waltz.

In $\frac{4}{4}$ and **C** the accents fall on the 1st and 3rd beats of the bar. The third beat is usually not quite as strong as the first, it is more of a 'medium' (M) accent:

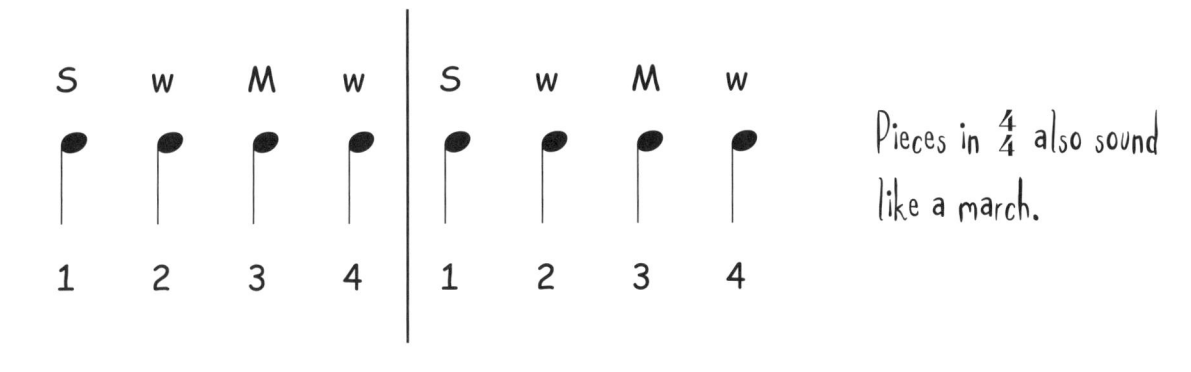

Pieces in $\frac{4}{4}$ also sound like a march.

Drawing Rests Correctly

Crotchet Rests

Think of the crotchet rest as starting off a bit like the letter 'Z' with the letter 'C' springing off the bottom. It must start in the top space and finish in the bottom space. Trace and draw some crotchet rests on this staff:

Minim Rests

Minim rests sit on the **third** line of the staff. They must not take up the whole space between the lines; draw them like this not like this !

Trace and draw some minim rests:

Whole Bar Rests (Semibreve Rests)

These hang from the fourth line and, like minim rests, must not take up the whole space! Trace and draw some here:

Quaver Rests

A quaver rest is like a curvy number '7'. It sits inside the middle two spaces. Try some:

The Anacrusis

An anacrusis is: "One or more unaccented notes before the first bar line" (how formal!).
Here are some rather famous examples of tunes with an anacrusis:

Hap - py BIRTH day to you, Hap - py birth day to you etc.

Aus - TRA - lians all let us re - joice etc.

We WISH you a mer-ry Christ-mas we wish you a mer-ry Christ-mas etc.

When you sing these, notice how the anacrusis is not accented.
It is the first beat of the first bar that is accented.

> The anacrusis is not a bar! Think of it as a beat that escaped from the last bar. A crotchet anacrusis means the last bar will be missing one crotchet beat.

The following rhythms begin with an anacrusis, but the last bar in each is WRONG - it has one too many beats. Can you write the same rhythm with a correct final bar?

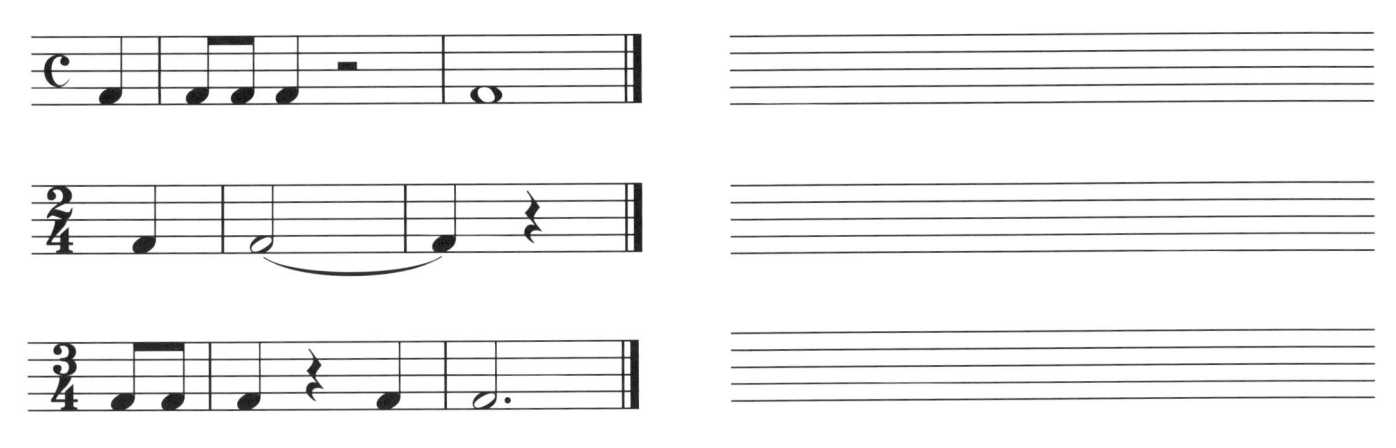

Adding Bar Lines

All you need to do is check the time signature and COUNT! Just a couple of handy tips:

★ Don't let ties and slurs (see p. 67) put you off - bar lines can cut through them.

★ Bar lines CANNOT cut through groups of quavers!

★ Watch out for the sneaky anacrusis (for instance, if the bar lines don't seem to fit properly).

1. Add bar lines to these melodies, including a double bar line at the end:

2. For these melodies you'll need to fill in the missing time signatures as well as some bar lines... tricky!

Grouping Rules

Quavers are usually grouped TWO at a time to show the crotchet beats e.g. ♫

Grouping quavers in pairs is the best way to do it for Grade 1 (in $\frac{2}{4}$, $\frac{3}{4}$, $\frac{4}{4}$ and **C**).

It is also correct to group 4 quavers together e.g. ♫♫, and this is what you will see in a lot of sheet music, BUT there is a very strict rule for this:

NEVER GROUP FOUR QUAVERS ON BEATS 2 AND 3!

(This is because you are not allowed to group two beats together if the first beat is weak.)

For instance, $\frac{4}{4}$ ♩♫♫♩ would be incorrect grouping of the quavers. The bar would have to be rewritten like this: $\frac{4}{4}$ ♩♫♫♩ . It sounds exactly the same!

Fill these bars with quavers correctly grouped (remember, it's easiest to group them in pairs for now):

$\frac{4}{4}$ _____ $\frac{3}{4}$ _____

$\frac{2}{4}$ _____   **C** _____

There is a similar rule for the minim rest (𝄼):

NEVER PUT A MINIM REST ON BEATS 2 AND 3! (A minim rest may not begin on a weak beat!)

So $\frac{4}{4}$ ♩ 𝄼 ♩ is wrong, and would have to be rewritten like this $\frac{4}{4}$ ♩ 𝄽 𝄽 ♩

To be safe, don't use minim rests AT ALL in $\frac{3}{4}$ - always use crotchet rests in $\frac{3}{4}$!

🔥 **HOT TIP:** Grouping is a bit like spelling. Words can be spelled differently but sound the same. Notes and rests must have the correct 'spelling' — it makes it much easier to read!

Groovy Grouping

Wrong	Why is it wrong?	Fix it up
3/4 (crotchet, minim rest)	The weak beats (beats 2 and 3) may not be grouped together into a minim rest	
2/4 (quaver, three beamed quavers)	Quavers must be grouped in twos - not singles or threes	
4/4 (crotchet, minim rest, crotchet rest)	Can't have minim rest on beats 2 and 3 - we must be able to see the strong beat on beat 3	
C (four beamed quavers, three beamed quavers, crotchet rest)	Can't have groups of four quavers on beats 2 and 3	
2/4 (minim rest)	Whole bar rest needed for a bar of silence - not minim rest	

The following melody has a grouping mistake in each bar. Can you rewrite it correctly on the stave below? (Remember, the SOUND must be the same, it will just LOOK different!)

Compose your own 4-bar rhythms here - with correct grouping, of course!

2/4

3/4

Completing the Bar

A very common test of rhythm is that you are given a bar without enough beats in it, and you have to complete it in a certain way. Just follow these steps:

1. Check how many beats are already in the bar.

2. Check the time signature and decide how many more beats are needed.

3. Make sure you read the question carefully... do you need to use **notes** or **rests?**

4. Fill up the bar remembering your **grouping rules.** (See page 53)

HOT TIP: Read the question very carefully! It asks you to complete the bar a certain way e.g. 'add one note' or 'use rests'. Don't get tricked!

1. Complete these bars with rests in the correct order. (Remember the rules for minim rests!)

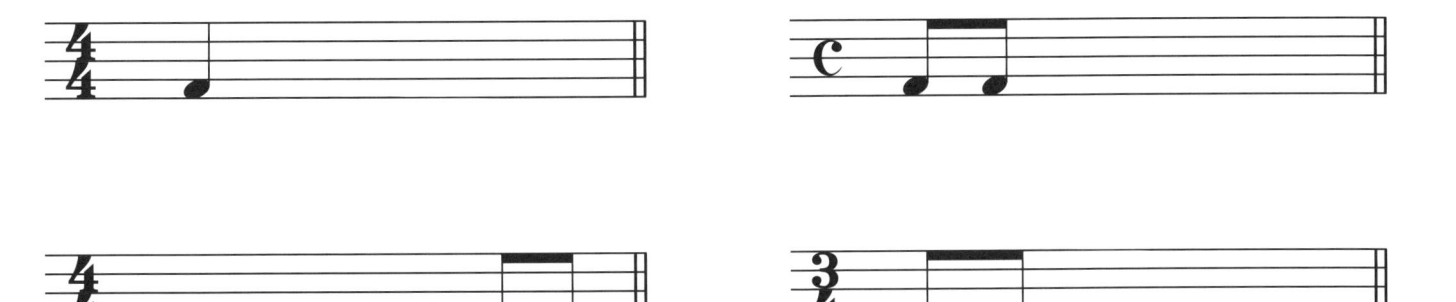

2. At each spot marked with an arrow, add one note to complete the bar. (Don't get tricked. The question asked for 'one note'... you can't use more than one note, and you can't use any rests!)

Handy Hint: Did you see the anacrusis??? Check your final bar!!!

Let's Complete More Bars

Hint: Read these questions very carefully!

1. At each place indicated by an arrow, write one note to complete the timing of the bar

2. Add a rest or rests to complete these bars:

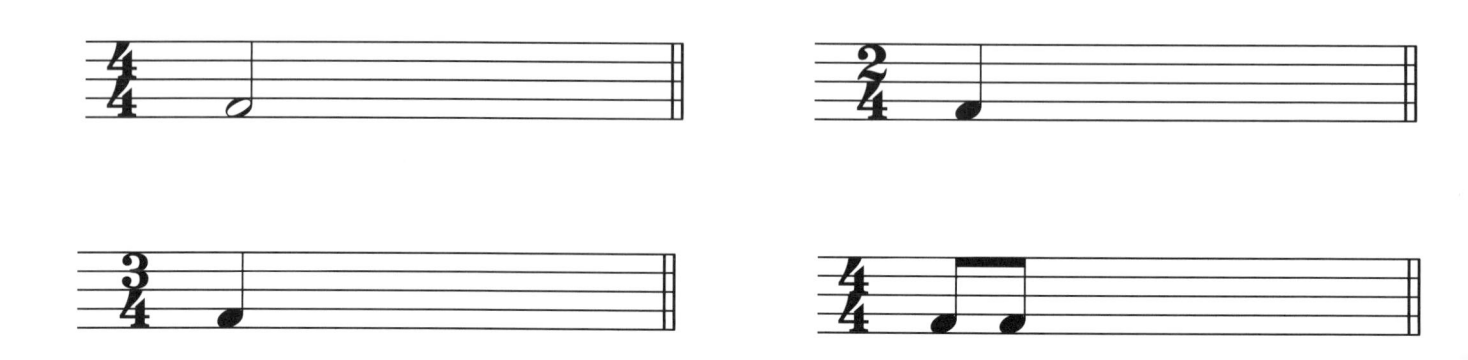

3. Complete these bars with quavers correctly grouped.

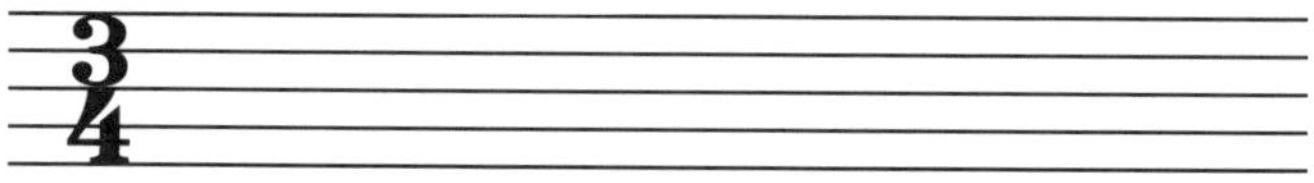

4. Add a rest at each place marked with an arrow to complete the timing of the bar.

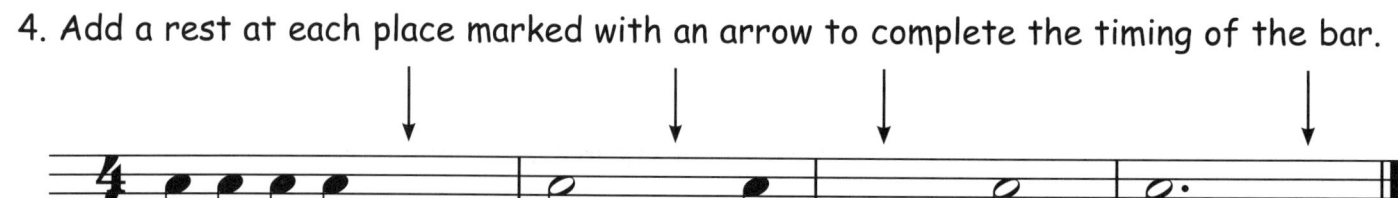

Warning: Check the wording of the above question!

Rhythmic Revision

1. Add bar lines (including a double bar line at the end) to the following:

2. How many crotchets are there in a minim? _____

3. How many minims are there in a semibreve? _____

4. Add the correct time signature to the following melodies:

5. Complete the following bars with a rest or rests in the correct order:

Another Test on Stuff

1. Can you find five mistakes in this melody? Circle them and then describe them below:

a) _____

b) _____

c) _____

d) _____

e) _____

/10

2. What's wrong with this G major key signature?

/1

_____

3. Write a scale that begins on the given note:

/5

- ★ write one octave descending
- ★ add the correct accidental
- ★ mark the semitones with a slur
- ★ complete the scale with a double bar line

4. What is an anacrusis? (See page 51 if you need to!) _____

/2

58

5. Rewrite this rhythm with correct grouping (one of the bars is actually correct!): /6

6. Number these scale degrees based on the key signature given: /9

7. Who wrote Chopin's 4th Ballade? (Just kidding but you should be able to answer this) _____ /1

8. Complete the following bars as directed: /6

1 rest   1 note and 1 rest   6 notes

Total: /40

Transposition

To transpose a melody is to put it into another key. It will have a new key signature and a whole new set of notes, but everything else stays the same!

Same

Time signature
Rhythm
Scale degree numbers
Shape
Phrasing (slurs)
Articulation (e.g. staccato)

Different

Key Signature
Notes (possibly stems too)

Ok, let's go! Follow the steps below to transpose this melody down into G major:

1. Name the key of the melody. _____

2. Write the scale degree numbers under the melody. (Revise p.37 if you need to!)

3. On the staff below, write the clef and **new** key signature of G major, then add the time signature.

4. The melody starts on scale degree no.1, so your new starting note will be scale degree no.1 of **G major**, which is ____. But which G will it be - high or low?

5. Take another look at the question - does it say to transpose 'up' or 'down'? ____ So your new melody starts **below** the original melody - easy!

6. Write the new melody, following the scale degree numbers.

7. Use the list above to check all the things that should be exactly the same!

More About Transposition

It's very common to be asked to transpose melodies that deliberately jump all over the place! Revise these checklists, then try the questions below.

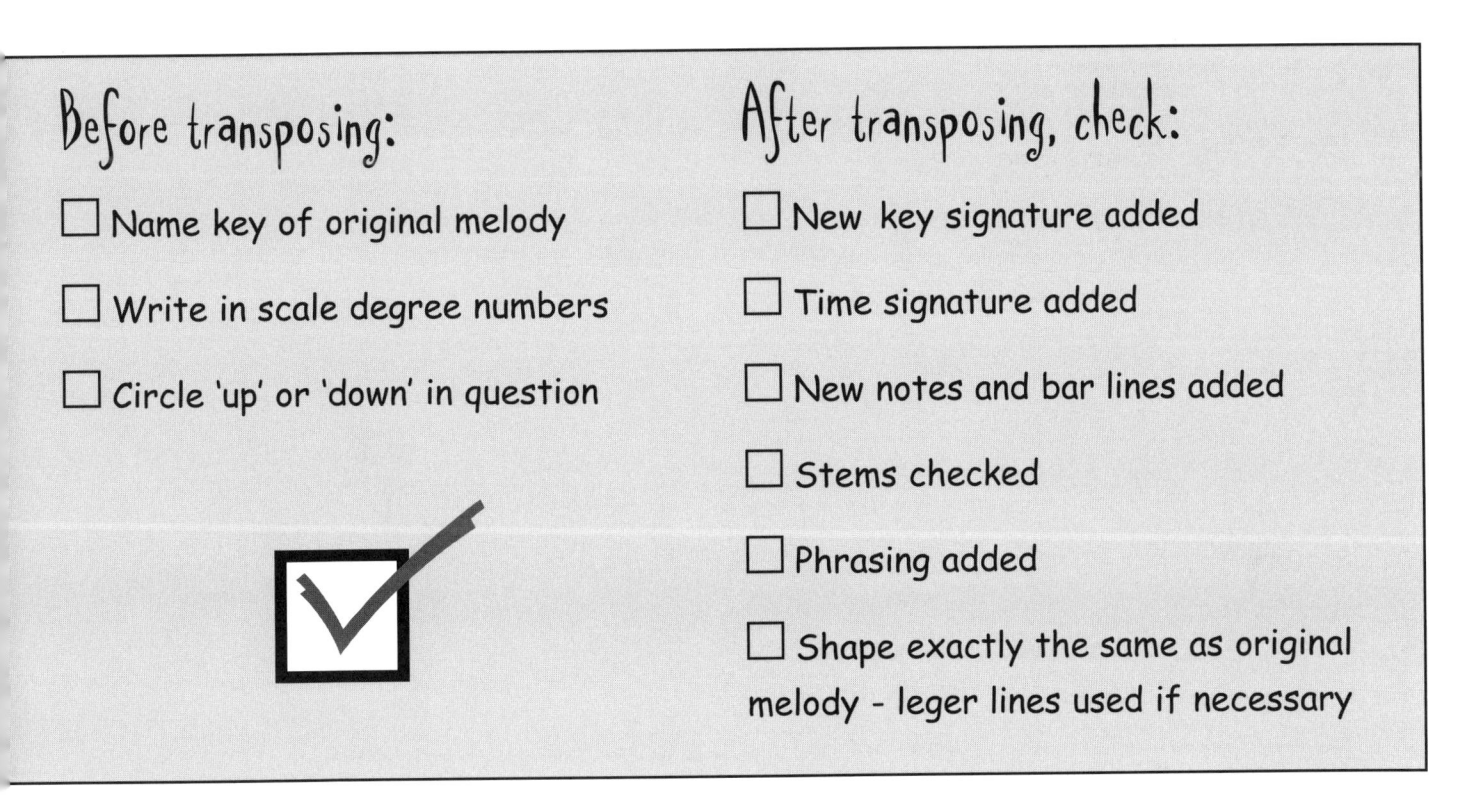

Before transposing:
- [ ] Name key of original melody
- [ ] Write in scale degree numbers
- [ ] Circle 'up' or 'down' in question

After transposing, check:
- [ ] New key signature added
- [ ] Time signature added
- [ ] New notes and bar lines added
- [ ] Stems checked
- [ ] Phrasing added
- [ ] Shape exactly the same as original melody - leger lines used if necessary

Transpose this melody up into F major. Use the checklists above!

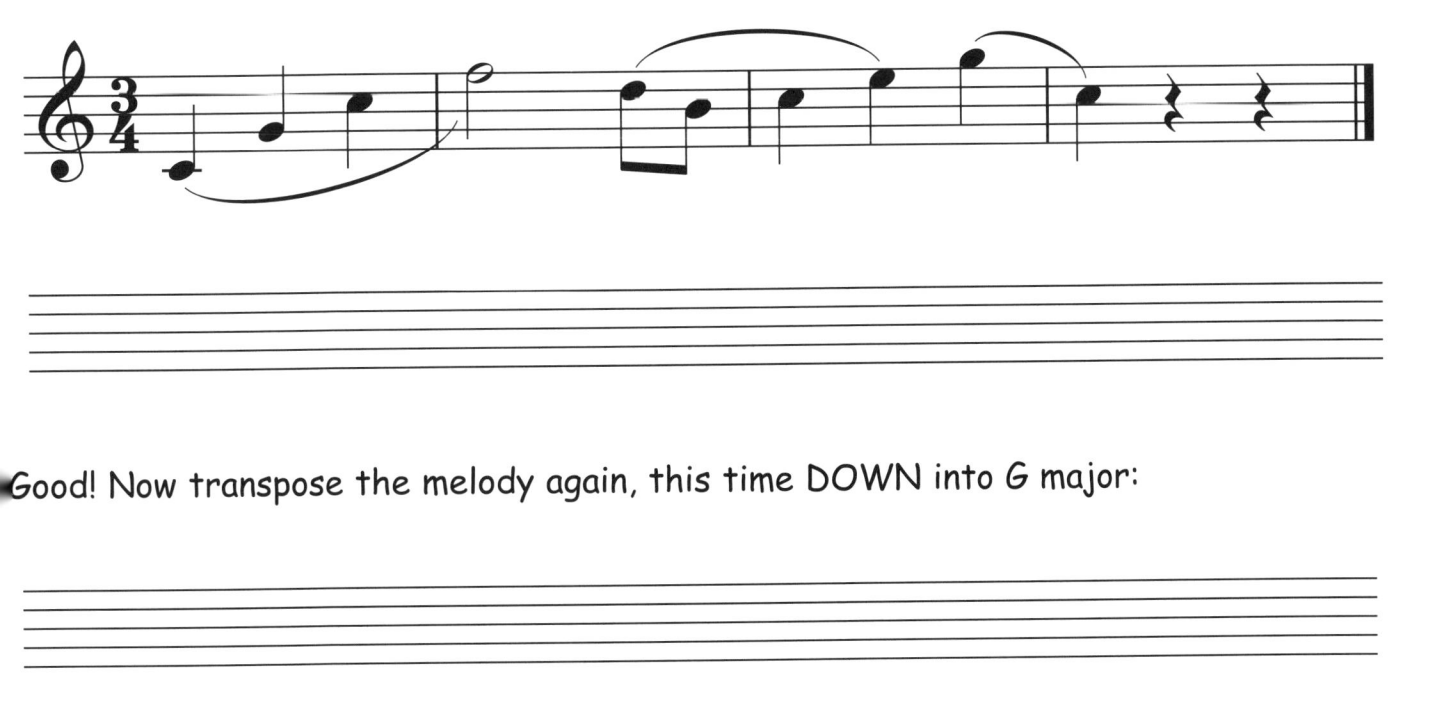

Good! Now transpose the melody again, this time DOWN into G major:

HOT TIP: Never try to transpose without writing scale degree numbers first!

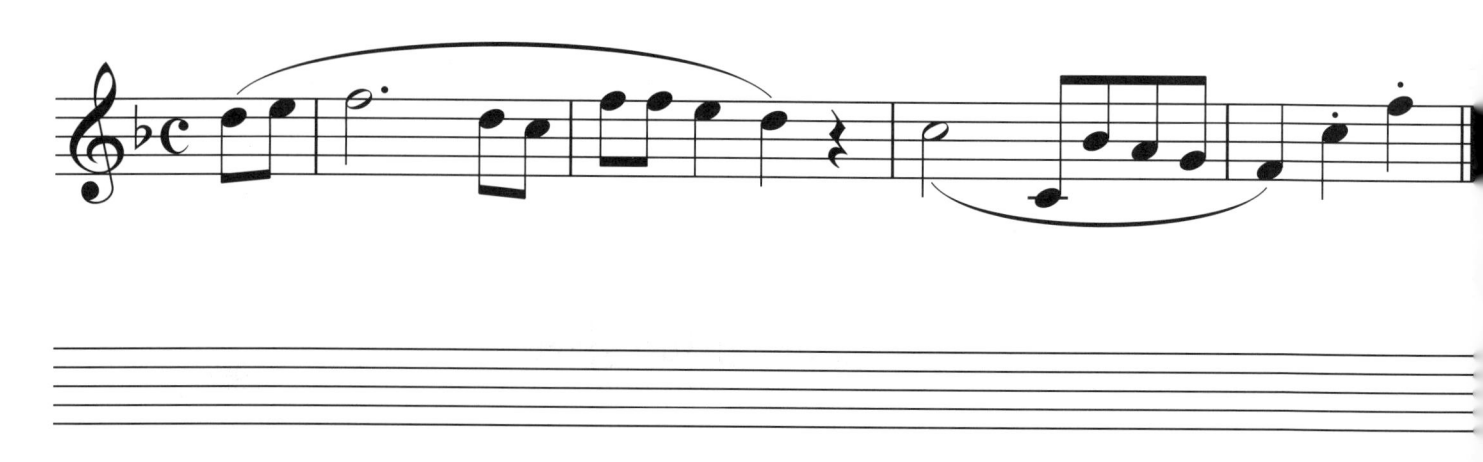

Let's Transpose

Transpose the following melody down into C major. Add the phrasing.

Transpose the following melody up into F major. Write the new key signature.

Transpose the following melody up into G major.

Transpose the following melody down into F major. Add the new key signature.

Transpose the following melody up into G major.

Transpose the following melody up into C major.

Remember to adjust your stems!!!

Answers for this workbook can be found at blitzbooks.com

Transposition and Other Things

1. Rewrite this melody with correct grouping and stems.

2. Now transpose it up into F major!

3. Finish these tonic triads (the tonic note is given) and add the correct key signature:

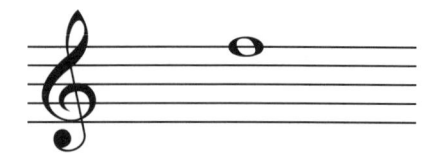

4. How many quavers are there in 3 minims? _____

5. Just for fun, name this note: _____

Word Search

This word search is different from most... the words hidden in the grid are actually the answers to the clues at the bottom of the page!

```
N I T S L O W E R S E T
O U L E N E D L D S R O
S E A E L E I P P I H N
I L E A G O G U A G W I
N L A S C E W D S H L C
U G N T G L R E O E R N
L A A L N I C L S H L P
N V C N I E E P I T R I
E O R S S B D M H N K A
E R U T A N G I S Y E K
L V S R R O R S C E I S
V I I U H D P C I C W L
M O S F P M I N I M A C
```

1. Which goes first after the clef: key signature or time signature?
2. Description of the time signature for 2 crotchet beats per bar.
3. On which line of the staff does the minim rest sit? Third/fourth/fifth
4. Another name for the 'semibreve' rest is the _____ ___ rest.
5. One or more beats before the first bar line.
6. Name for scale degree no. 1.
7. Proper name for distance of an 8th.
8. Which note in a major scale is no. 1, lowest or highest?
9. Number of tones in a major scale.
10. Short lines used for notes above or below the staff.
11. An interval where both notes are exactly the same pitch.
12. 'Rall' and 'Rit' both mean to become gradually _____ . (See next page!)
13. You won't find a _____ rest in Simple Duple or Simple Triple time.
14. Collective name for sharps, flats and naturals.
15. Chord consisting of three notes.

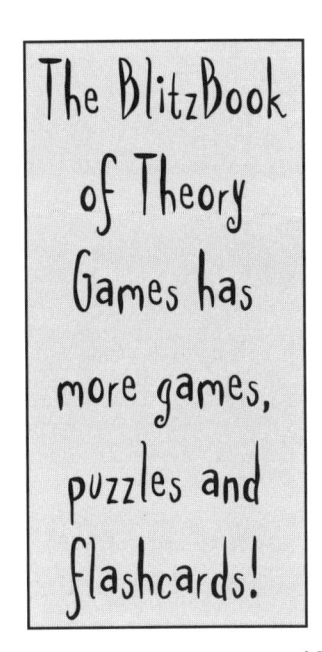

The BlitzBook of Theory Games has more games, puzzles and flashcards!

Italian Terms

Adagio	-	slowly
Andante	-	at an easy walking pace
Moderato	-	at a moderate speed
Allegro	-	lively and fast
Presto	-	very fast
Accelerando (accel.)	-	gradually becoming faster
Rallentando (rall.)	-	gradually becoming slower
Ritardando (rit. / ritard.)	-	gradually becoming slower
Ritenuto (riten. / rit.)	-	immediately slower
A tempo	-	return to former speed
Crescendo (cresc.)	-	gradually becoming louder
Decrescendo (decresc.)	-	gradually becoming softer
Diminuendo (dim.)	-	gradually becoming softer
*Forte (**f**)*	-	loud
*Piano (**p**)*	-	soft
Legato	-	smooth, well connected
Staccato	-	short and detached

HOT TIP: There are heaps of 'gradually becoming' words... don't get them mixed up!

Other Signs and Definitions

Sign	Name	Meaning
$<$	Crescendo	Gradually becoming louder
$>$	Decrescendo/Diminuendo	Gradually becoming softer
♩. or ♩	Staccato	Short and detached
f	Forte	Loud ('f' always written lower case)
p	Piano	Soft ('p' always written lower case)
(slur notation)	Slur	Play smoothly (can be over two or more notes)
(tie notation)	Tie	Play the first note and hold for value of both
(bar line)	Bar line	Divides music into equal sections according to the time signature
(double bar line)	Double bar line	Indicates the end of a piece or important section

Add staccato signs to the rest of these notes (notice how the dot goes in the space nearest the note head)

★ Add a **sign** to show that the first 4 notes should become gradually louder.

★ Add a **sign** to show that the last 6 notes should become gradually softer.

★ Add a **sign** to show that the notes in bar 2 should be played forte.

Timed Test II

Time:

Time yourself doing this quiz. Do it as fast as you can, then record your finishing time above. But... guess what? Your teacher will **ADD ON 10 SECONDS** for every mistake you make! It's fun to go fast, but more important to be **accurate**. Good luck!

1. Name two Italian terms that mean 'gradually becoming softer':

   _____ and _____

2. What does 'staccato' mean? _____

3. Add a time signature and the missing bar lines to this melody:

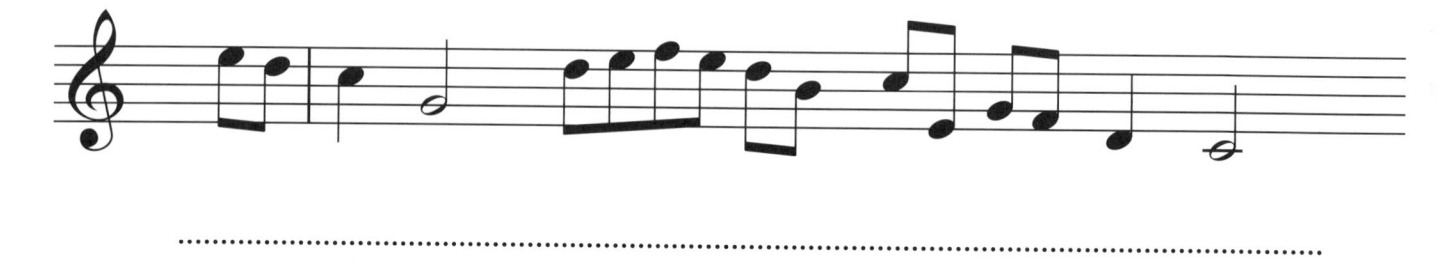

4. Now write the correct scale degree numbers under each note!

5. Why did the chicken cross the road? (ok you don't really have to answer this) _____

6. Fill in this grid:

Sign	Name of Sign	Meaning of Sign

STOP THE CLOCK - FILL IN YOUR TIME AT THE TOP!

☐ I made no mistakes! I keep my time of _____ !

☐ I made _____ mistakes. My new time is _____ .

More About Signs

You will often come across questions which ask you to add terms and signs to given melodies. This is a test of your overall knowledge, so the questions are designed to really make you think! For example, here are two different instructions:

Add a sign to become gradually softer

Add a sign to play the phrase softly

See? Quite tricky! There is a big difference between the sign for 'gradually becoming softer' (=====—) and the sign for 'softly' (p)

Check out this question:

Add a sign to raise the pitch of the 'B' by one semitone

Your first reaction might be to raise the B with a sharp sign. **But wait** - there is a B flat in the key signature! What sign will you need instead? Add this in now.

One final example of tricky questions:

Add ties in the appropriate places in this melody

'Appropriate places' (a rather huge phrase!) basically means that you need to find the right spots. You may only add a tie between two notes of the **same pitch**. Try it now!

HOT TIP: 'Signs' are symbols, not words. The only abbreviations of Italian terms regarded as signs are 'f' for forte and 'p' for piano.

Let's Practise Adding Stuff

Handy Hint: When answering questions like these, give as much information as possible, and make sure that you write all your 'meanings' in English!

To the following melody, add:

i) The correct clef.
ii) The missing time signature.
iii) Signs to show the notes in the first bar are short and detached.
iv) A crotchet rest on the first beat of bar 2.
v) A sign to raise the pitch of the note in bar 2.
vi) A tie in bar 3.
vii) The missing stem in bar 4.
viii) A sign to show the melody gets gradually softer in bar 5.

Study this melody:

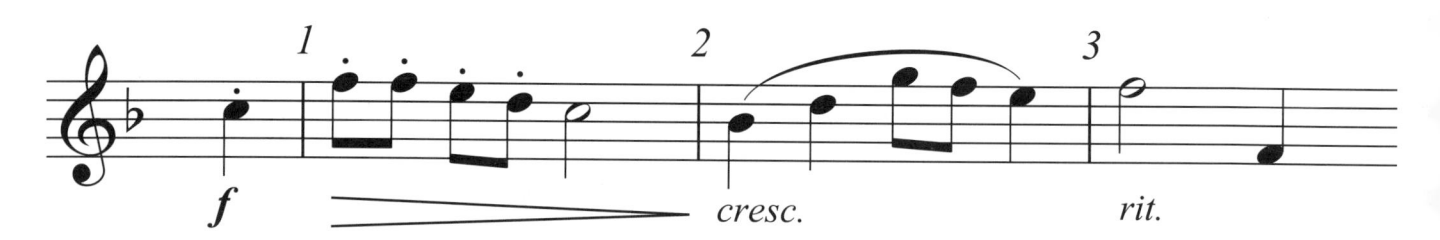

i) What key is it in? _____
ii) Add an Italian term above the first note to show the melody should be played slowly.
iii) Does it get faster or slower at the end? _____ (Warning: do not simply answer 'yes')
iv) How should the quavers in bar 1 be played? _____
v) Does the melody begin loudly or softly? _____
vi) Give the meaning of the Italian abbreviation in bar 2. _____
vii) Add a sign to show the melody is finished.
viii) Add the correct time signature.

Final Revision Test (Phew!)

1. Rewrite this melody with correct stems and grouping. /7

2. Now transpose it down to C major! /10

3. To your **newly transposed** C major melody, add: /4

   ★ A sign to show it begins softly

   ★ A sign to raise the pitch of the F in bar 1

   ★ A sign to show the first 2 bars should be played smoothly

   ★ A tie in an appropriate place

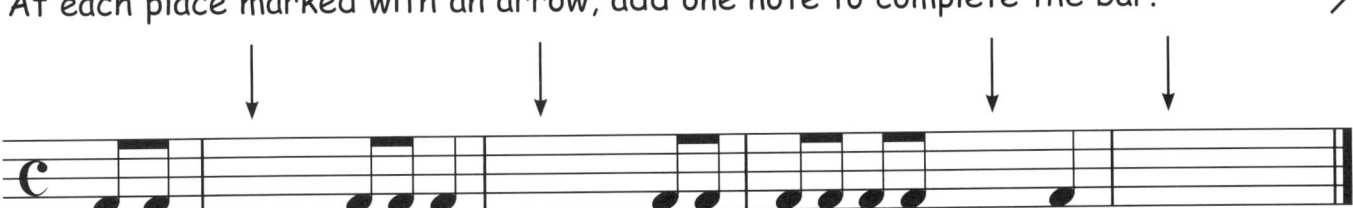

4. At each place marked with an arrow, add one note to complete the bar. /4

Total: /25

Mad Multiple Choice

1. Legato means:
   - A. smooth and detached
   - B. short and well connected
   - C. smooth and well connected

2. This note is:
   - A. E sharp
   - B. E
   - C. E natural

3. Accidentals go:
   - A. to the left (before)
   - B. to the right (after)
   - C. underneath

4. Circle the best treble clef:

5. G major has:
   - A. a B flat
   - B. 4 sharps
   - C. an F sharp

6. Semitones fall between:
   - A. 3-4 and 5-6
   - B. 3-4 and 7-8
   - C. 9-10 and 11-12

7. Circle the correct way to draw a 3rd:

8. Name this interval:    A. 17th
   B. 1st
   C. 8ve

9. When writing scale degree numbers under **melodies**:
   A. we only use numbers 1-7
   B. we don't use number 8
   C. A and B

10. Name this sign:    A. Slur
    B. Tie
    C. Staccato

11. Circle the correct way to draw a B flat:

12. Quavers should be grouped: A. in twos
    B. in eights
    C. in threes

13. We should learn our Italian terms because:
    A. the teacher told us to
    B. we should understand what they mean in the music we play
    C. we might visit Italy one day

14. Circle the correct way to write a 7th above G:

73

15. What's wrong with this leger line note?

    A.   The top leger line is unnecessary
    B.   The circle is too small
    C.   Nothing, it's perfect

16. The sign ⟩ means:
    A.   crescendo
    B.   gradually becoming softer
    C.   all of the above

17. Presto means:
    A.   fast
    B.   very fast
    C.   extremely fast

18. A double bar line means:
    A.   the end of a piece
    B.   the beginning of a piece
    C.   the end of a piece or important section

19. You should not use minim rests in:
    A. $\frac{2}{4}$
    B. $\frac{3}{4}$
    C. $\frac{4}{4}$

(Hint: There are two correct answers to question 19!)

20. Middle C lives:
    A.   above the bass staff
    B.   below the treble staff
    C.   A and B

Test Paper... sort of

All theory books end with a test paper, but this one is DIFFERENT. It already has the answers in it (mostly wrong answers!) and your job is to be the teacher - you have to **mark** it.

When you've found all the mistakes, go to **blitzbooks.com** and download the EXACT SAME PAPER - this time with no answers already in it. See if you can get 100%!

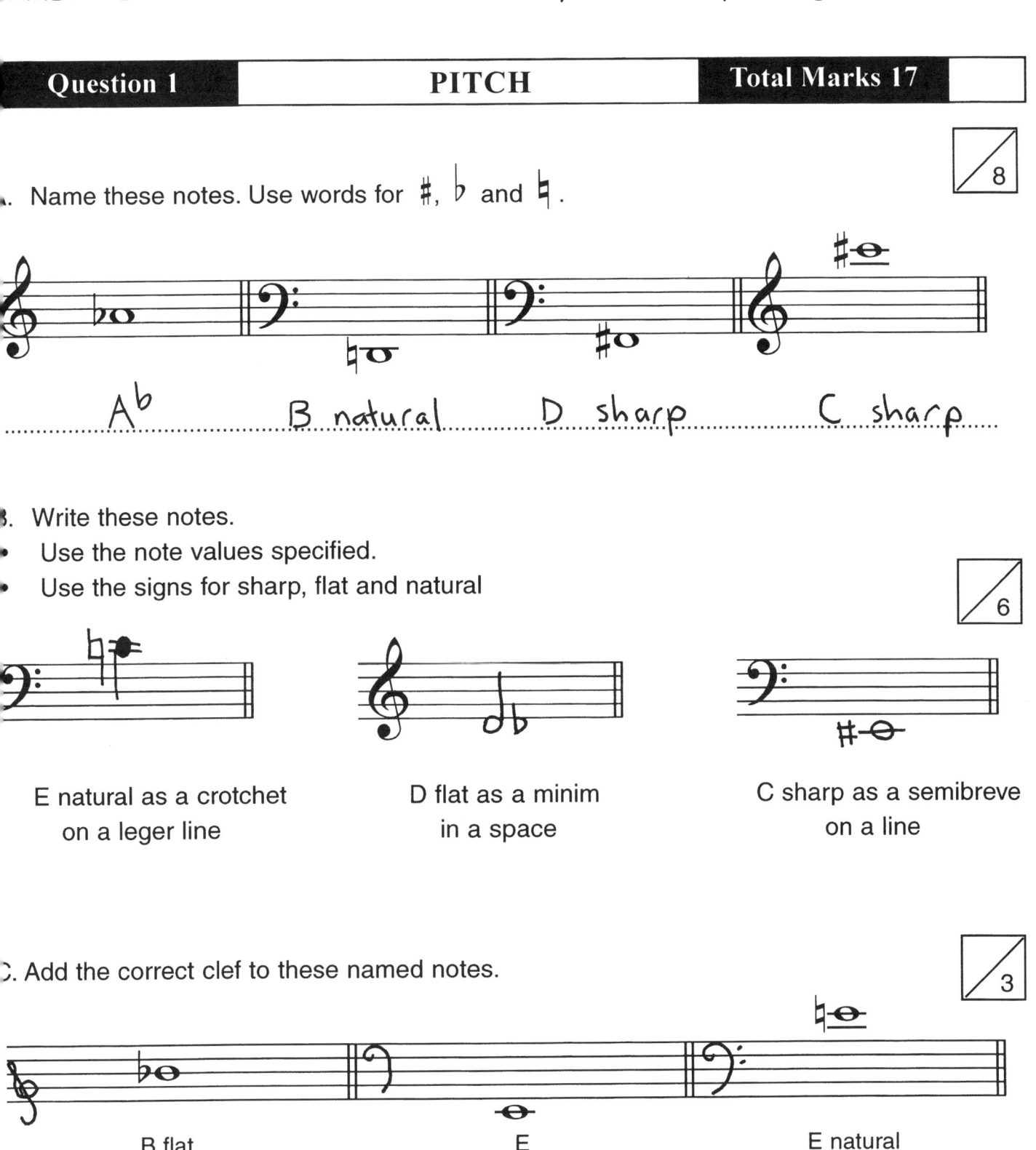

| **Question 1** | **PITCH** | **Total Marks 17** |

A. Name these notes. Use words for ♯, ♭ and ♮. /8

A♭   B natural   D sharp   C sharp

B. Write these notes.
- Use the note values specified.
- Use the signs for sharp, flat and natural /6

E natural as a crotchet on a leger line

D flat as a minim in a space

C sharp as a semibreve on a line

C. Add the correct clef to these named notes. /3

B flat   E   E natural

Page 1 / Theory Grade 1

| Question 2 | KEYS and SCALES | Total Marks 21 |

A. Write the scale of F major.

- Use the treble clef
- Use accidentals
- Write one octave descending
- Use crotchets
- Mark each tone with a slur
- Complete the scale with a double bar line

/6

B. Add a clef and any accidentals necessary to make this the scale of G major.

/3

C. Name this scale and mark the semitones.

/3

Name: ...... C major ......

D. Write the correct scale degree numbers under the notes of this melody.

/9

6   4   2   1   6   4   7   3   6

Page 2 / Theory Grade 1

Question 3 — INTERVALS AND CHORDS — Total Marks 15

A. Write these intervals above the given tonic notes. /4

      7th   8ve   2nd   4th

B. Name these intervals by number only. /4

4   2   7   8

C. Is this interval a 4th? /1
Yes or No? ...Think so......

D. Write these tonic triads with their key signatures. /6

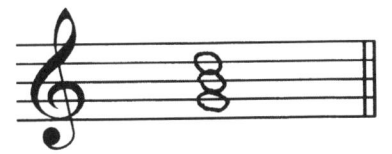

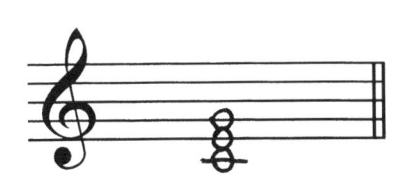

    G major   F major   C major

Page 3 / Theory Grade 1

Question 4 **TIME and RHYTHM** **Total Marks 18**

A. Complete each bar as directed. /6

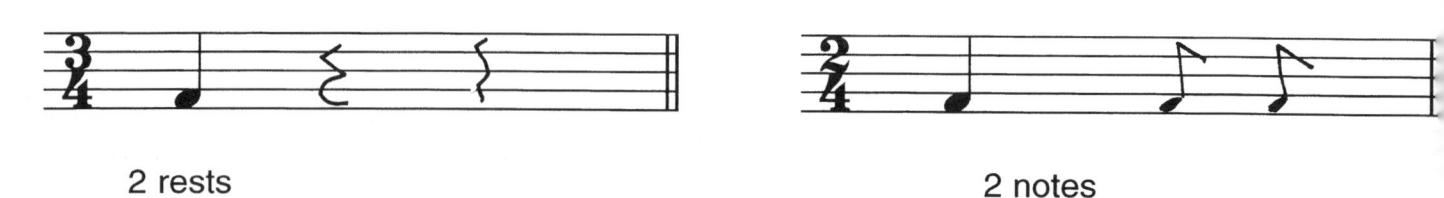

2 rests

2 notes

1 note 1 rest

B. Use two notes to complete each of these bars. /6

C. Complete the following bars using quavers correctly grouped. /4

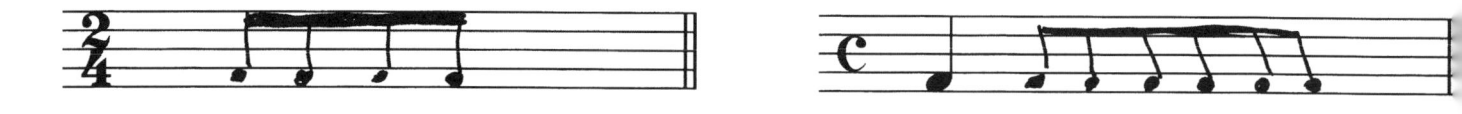

D. Add the correct time signature to these rhythms /2

Page 4 / Theory Grade 1

| Question 5 | **TRANSPOSITION** | Total Marks 12 |

Transpose this melody down into F major.

| Question 6 | **TERMS AND SIGNS** | Total Marks 17 |

A. Give the English meaning of the following terms or signs. /7

i) *ritenuto* ..... getting immediately slower
ii) *rall.* ..... getting slower
iii) *moderato* ..... moderate
iv) *adagio* ..... extremely slow
v) staccato
vi) crescendo

N.B. In the uncompleted version of this test paper (blitzbooks.com), questions A and B appear in the opposite order.

B. Study the melody then answer the questions below.

Allegro

[Musical staff with melody in 3/4 time, F major, marked *p*, bars 1-8, with crescendo under bar 7 and "loudly" written under bar 8]

i. Name the key of the melody. F major

ii. What is the meaning of the Italian Term at the beginning? Fast

iii. Add a sign to show the quavers in bar 3 should be played smoothly.

iv. Add signs to show the quavers in bar 7 should be played short and detached.

v. Explain the time signature. It means 3/4

vi. Does this melody contain any ties? Yes or no? Not sure

vii. Explain the sign under bar 7. getting louder

viii. Why are there only two beats in the last bar? Because the composer forgot to finish

ix. Add a sign to show that the last bar should be played loudly.

x. Add a sign to show the that the melody is finished.

Mark /100

How did you go marking this paper? Did you find lots of mistakes? It's a good idea to discuss all of them with your teacher. Talk about WHY some mistakes might happen e.g. not checking the clef, or not completing the question. Understanding the mistakes in this paper will really help you when you go on to try the same paper yourself. Now go to blitzbooks.com and download the uncompleted version. Good luck!